THE HEALING POWER OF GRIEF

The Healing Power of
GRIEF

JACK SILVEY MILLER

A CROSSROAD BOOK
THE SEABURY PRESS • NEW YORK

Second Printing

1978
The Seabury Press
815 Second Avenue
New York, N.Y. 10017

Printed in the United States of America

Library of Congress Cataloging in Publication Data
Miller, Jack Silvey.   The healing power of grief.
"A Crossroad book."
1. Grief. 2. Death. 1. Title.
BJ1487.M54   152.4'43   78-16882   ISBN 0-8164-0402-X

For all the saints
living and dead of
The Presbyterian Church
Mt. Kisco, New York

I am quite ready to acknowledge that I ought to be grieved at death if I were not persuaded that I am going to the gods who are wise and good (of this I am as certain as I can be of any such matters) and to men departed who are better than those whom I leave behind.

—Socrates

Every time I have a heart attack I get a lump in my throat and I get scared, and all of a sudden I hear this voice inside of me saying, 'You'll be all right, man, calm down. I'll live with you, I'll die with you, and I'll take care of you no matter what.' And you know what? That lump in my throat, it just goes away.

—Tod Dodson

CONTENTS

Preface

THIS BOOK BEGAN, in a way, with the crib death of my sister Mary Kathleen. Until then my own days had seemed immortal but from that hour my nights were sweating crises over the cruelty of death. What was it like to die? Would it hurt? Why did it have to happen to perfectly good and innocent people? I concluded that death was something "wrong" with life, the one and greatest breakdown in the human condition that needed to be "fixed."

The years that followed brought an extraordinary number of untimely deaths to me. All deaths, of course, are untimely to someone, but these happened so often and to so many young people that they threatened my own right to live forever. Either I had to face it and come to terms with the facts of the universe, or go on running from fear of the inevitable. Yet if I did run away, it finally occurred to me, death wouldn't. So began the logical process of growing up and thinking through what death meant—psychologically, philosophically, and theologically.

Though the reason escapes me now, I once was asked to stand guard over a dead body. All through the night revelation became brighter and brighter until I found myself actually rejoicing. Previously I had confused two frightening issues until they became one and the same—funerals and death. Not only are they not married to each other, but they haven't even met! That dead body beside me had nothing to do with the personality, the spirit, the essence of my comrade. I had mistaken embalming and cosmetic coverage, closing coffin lids and graveyard excavations with the death event.

I later came to discover the reason for and importance of funerals and memorial services. They were never again to cast a negating shadow on the truly natural event which we call death.

It *is* an event, I finally affirm. And I do so with triumph and gladness. We do not go gently into that final night, for to my mind it is neither night nor is it something which renders us passive victims. We participate in a mysterious way and we are not left powerless or impotent in the last event for which the first was made. In a fashion unknown to mortal mind, our insatiable longing for perfection is at last quenched. It is a state for which we all strive on this earth, a state which never completely comes to any of us. We go on searching for more. When a reporter asked John D. Rockefeller how much money it would take to make him perfectly happy, he replied, "Just a little bit more." Only the death event calms the inner craving for completion and wholeness, for the perfection of all that is alive within us.

Just what form it will take I do not know. We've all heard plenty of theories. Mark Twain used to say he thought it strange that so many people looked forward to heaven and playing harps eternally when not a single one of them showed enough interest to sign up for lessons on earth. During my blatantly unsuccessful athletic career, a classmate ventured the notion that when I got to paradise I would play on God's baseball team. That was doubtless his interpretation of heaven. It was my idea of hell. So, too, everyone has his or her own idea of the pleasures of life hereafter. For my own part, I will be relieved to be perfected by the love of the Almighty. Considering the material He has to work with, that will indeed be a miracle worth waiting for. And it's surely not too much to believe. If God can pull off so many of the wonder-filled miracles which touch our daily lives (green leaves from seemingly dead branches, morning's glory from night's grip), He should have little problem in bringing off the final coup of my being. So I go on believing in a death event which is eternally alive and of which we will be deeply aware—not because of a love I have never known but rather because of a love I have always known. Gladly will I count myself among the cheaters about such things as this life ahead of us. I have it on good report from the One who has been there and who came back to plant eternity in the human heart: "In my Father's house there are many great things. If it were not so, I would have told you." At long last death—as a passive and permanent end to life—has lost its sting. And the grave—that hole in the ground that has no earthly exit—has lost its victory. And I am free.

What of hell? To my mind, hell is not believing in any of these possibilities. Hell is living hopelessly in the face of a conquering death and then dying in the bottomless pit of nothingness. No world without end, and no Amen!

The people unfolding before you in the pages that follow are real. They did and said what I have set down. Not one of them was trying to be a hero or speak the last and right words. Some of them, in their dying, taught me about the indefatigable and undefeatable spirit of living. And some of them, in their living, have convinced me of the glorious surprises surrounding the miracle of death. All of them have been my guides—those who have gone before me and those who have remained with me while we grieve together. Our community of saints, living and dead, is testimony that the gates of hell shall not prevail against us. We can endure. We can survive. And we can take up hope again.

This book is not actually about death. It is about the long and solitary process of grieving after it. No two people will experience all of the stages and phases in the same way or to the same degree. Just as no one ever loves quite the way anyone else loves, neither will anyone ever grieve quite the way another grieves. But here I intend to paint a simple portrait of the universal and yet profoundly personal stories of my clay-footed friends who have come through the valley of the shadow of death.

Bob James, in his unflinching way, kept inspiring me to write this book. Following him, his spirited mother kept encouraging me to finish it. Like the God who sustained all of us through the deep pain and quiet joy, she kept at me until I could not quit. She corrected my mortal typing, wiped away my sinful commas, and smiled on all my misspelling. Now she, too, must take up battle with the same disease and we have sounded our own call to arms. We're going to go on embracing the universe in all its mysterious ways, laughing at the things we used to fear, ringing the joy out of every minute, and living in faith. We cannot have it any other way.

CHAPTER 1

Why Mine?

IT WAS THE BEST of all possible days. Jeff and Mary, their red heads brightened by the sunlight streaming in through the church window, had brought their baby to be baptized. I remember being nervous because it was one of my first baptisms, and Jeff and Mary were close personal friends. Baptism is traditionally the day when the parents announce to the world the Christian name of their child. I finished the charge to the couple and then asked the traditional question: "And what have you named the baby?"

"We have named her Rebecca Sarah."

"Rebecca Sarah Smith, I baptize thee in the name of the Father, the Son, and the Holy Spirit. Amen."

Almost two years later Mary called from their new home in San Francisco. "Becky died in the night. Can you come right away?"

I took a night flight from New York. It gave me hours to try and make sense of this hell. But there was no sense to be made of it. There never is. I fought for words to speak at the service which might put things into a larger, more comforting perspective, but no words came. At least, not enough. Not enough to salve the wound of a lost child.

There's nothing more contrary to the scheme of things than for a mother to bury her child. We bury our parents when they have had their three score years and ten, and this is difficult enough. But to bury our children flies in the face of nature herself. It rips into our guts and tears at our hearts as nothing else on earth can do. Life was not created to come to this.

As the jet flew west, I kept thinking of the other mothers I had known who had lost their children. I thought of Kay's mother who used to sit and cry at her bedside, trying to do needlepoint and hoping for some sign of new life. The sign never came. But at least she had time to prepare for the death. Kay was only twenty-four, but her strange disease had taken years finally to win the battle. There is a silent knowing, in the heart, that the child must die and so the grief process begins before the death event.

I thought of Tod's mother, Jean. Tod was twenty-four and had grown up knowing that some day he would have an early heart attack, and it would be his last. Never sickly, he was just a little slow. Sundays he assisted me at the church with the teenagers and during the week did volunteer work at the hospital. Long before he died he accepted his own death and talked about it openly. He wanted to make sure that two teenagers would inherit his eyes. And he wanted his body to go to science so that his lifelong illness could be studied and understood. He wanted to make a contribution with what life he had to offer. His father couldn't bring himself to believe the facts; his mother came early to accept them. She would lose her only son and she was preparing for it.

I thought of my two young friends back in New York who were still dying of cancer and multiple sclerosis. Were their parents facing the facts, or were they blocking the inevitable so as to survive the painful days? No matter how hard one tries, the facts keep hitting harder and harder. Everyone has a coping mechanism, a built-in shock absorber, that protects and yet lets the truth of it all seep through, gradually and tenderly.

Jeff and Mary had no warning. They weren't prepared to give up their baby. I knew we would be starting from square one and that Mary would ask the ancient question to which there is no answer. "Why mine?" And I knew that I would be left without words of comfort. My prayer, flying west, was that my presence, our friendship, would be enough to sustain us through the days ahead. We were all we had to offer each other and, somehow, we would have to be enough.

We were sitting in the kitchen of their small apartment when she asked it. "Why Becky?" She was still in shock. The truly great questions of life have no answers but we have to ask them. We have to cry out in the full face of the dark universe and beg the heavens for an answer—"Why mine?"

I remember exactly what I said because the words just kept coming, almost as if they were being written and handed over to me as quickly as I could speak. "God isn't in the business of causing grief. He didn't cause Becky to die, but He *cares* that she died. There's a difference. God doesn't get up in the morning and sort through evil to bring on the human race for the day. He doesn't plan to take a baby in California and a teenager in New York. He doesn't will that we should suffer, but in our suffering He cares for us and wants to get near us. If we're open, Mary, He will come, even in the darkest night, and stand with us. He lost a son, too."

Theologically, that makes good sense. It is the very purpose and plan of the cross of Christianity, that God can identify with the very worst of the human condition. Death. And the rest of the story is the very hope of life. That we were not born for the grave. Theologically, that makes good sense. But Mary needed more than words and theology. So we sat up through the night, crying and talking, even laughing at certain memories.

The Calvary Presbyterian Church of San Francisco gave us the use of its small chapel. Some friends from New York joined us and new friends the Smiths had made in California came along. I remember thinking that day that our church was a true church just then. We had spanned a continent with our love.

What follows is a mortal's attempt to deal with the things we mortals will never completely understand.

— IN MEMORIAM —
Rebecca Sarah Smith

Almost two years ago, we stood together in our church in New York and welcomed Rebecca into our circle of concern—and through us, into God's active concern. That circle of concern is never broken by death. Rather, it takes on the light of the divine so that those who are absent from our community live in our hearts as the saints of God.

Rebecca will always be a part of your family. She will forever be a part of our circle of love—and no power on earth can change that. Not even death. She did not live in vain. All the laughter and motion she brought into this world will remain perfectly etched at the heart of your home life.

The pain and emptiness you are feeling now is proof enough that Rebecca lived a full measure of love among those she touched. That love will not die—it can only grow stronger as the pain subsides and the memories become filled with sunlight and health. When you gather as a family, speak of her, speak of her again, because God would not have her left out of your lives. He would not have you victims of death.

I keep thinking of your remark, Jeff, that Becky was so full of life, so innocent and pure and vital. Death cannot deny that. Through faith, it can only affirm that life. Regardless of the years and events ahead of us all, Becky is affirmed always in the innocence of her youth. Age will take its toll from those of us who stretch our days into threescore years and ten. Compromise and evil will leave their mark on us as people who must sometimes struggle to survive. But Becky will always be the perfection of young life—the perfection of innocence and vitality.

My sadness is that she cannot be known to the world years from now. But my certainty is that she will always be known to you as a sacred treasure. No power on earth can separate you from such a treasure. So, in that very special way, you can take heart that her life was not in vain. She will live always in your family.

There's a piece of advice ministers usually give to families who are grieved. It goes something like this: "Don't plague yourself with the question 'Why did it happen?' because there is no answer. Instead, fill your minds with thanksgiving for the life you shared."

It may be good and true advice, but it's not honest enough for us. I know you too well to think you'll never wonder why, or curse the darkness that's bound to overtake you from time to time. So I'll just say: at times like that, be honest enough not just to confront the mystery of the universe, but to confront the God beyond that universe. If you find yourselves crying in the darkness, go even further and cry to the God who indwells the darkness. He hears you. When you and I point to the tragedies of this world and wonder "Why?" it is God who meets us and points to the cross: "I too have suffered Death. I too have cried out against the evil and injustice of it all." That cross tells me that God does not cause death, nor does He protect us from it, but He cares for us in death, and points always to life. It was the same God who spoke beyond the empty tomb and said, "Come, follow me, and have life."

"In my father's house there are many forms of being—I go to prepare a place for you, that where I am there you will be also." Something tells me it's true, Jeff and Mary. I believe it. Have you read the research on death and dying Dr. Kubler-Ross has done? In her last book she makes this notation to physicians, nurses, families: "When I began my work several years ago, I was not aware of any signs of life beyond death. Now, after thousands of conversations with dying patients, I'm convinced, without doubt, that there is life beyond the grave."

It seems too much for mortal minds to believe. But I believe it. And I've a feeling the more you experience this little heart that never stops beating in your heart, the more you reach beyond the agonizing questions to this mysterious being we call God within us, the more you will believe it too. God has set eternity in the heart—even God has suffered Death—and turned it into life. This, then, is the quiet good news of Christ's healing presence in your loss. He heals through the circle of concern His church sends to you. He heals through the circle of your family's love— that circle which will never be broken, only strengthened. And He heals through His own death, which turns into life for us all.

Mary, I've thought about our conversation last night. You're right, we've become so isolated from the facts of life in modern times. Medical science and progress have kept us from seeing truth. But the facts still remain. We are mortal. We are from the dust—and to dust we shall return. But through faith, the essence of life is eternal. It takes the wings of the morning, the wings of quiet peace and understanding. It takes the wings of a little angel forever in you, and in your God.

Amen.

There's an old nursery rhyme I like at times like this; it's just right for the benediction of little girls:

> Matthew, Mark, Luke and John,
> The bed be blest that I lie on.
> Four angels to my bed,
> Four angels round my head,
> One to watch and one to pray,
> And two to bear my soul away.

We wanted the last rite to be private. Becky was cremated and we wanted to go away somewhere alone to scatter the ashes. There's a time for friends to gather around, and a time to be alone in the soul.

We decided on Mount Tamalpais. I stopped at a street vendor's in San Francisco and bought up all his daffodils. We drove from the city out to the mountain and up its craggy side. Then we hiked up what seemed like miles of crooked paths until we came to the place. In the Old Testament, every great event and happening was marked at 'the place'. There was always to be a mark on the earth to commemorate what life had brought to pass. We found ours beneath a gnarled, bushy tree that looked for all the world like an olive tree. Somehow, we knew this was the place. Mary named the tree Becky's tree. I arranged the daffodils around its base, putting them in sunshine so their bright yellow faces would remind us of life. Mary opened the box of ashes.

It must have been the sight of ashes and bone: ashes to ashes, dust to dust. She began wailing with a mournful sound I had heard before but couldn't quite recall when. She threw herself into Jeff's arms and the two of them stood there on the plank of that great mountain, their bright red hair highlighted as it had been the day they first brought Becky to the church.

I moved away and remembered. She was making the sound of a mother cow which has just been separated from her calf. It was weaning time and no mother on earth can take it naturally. At least not suddenly. Mary moaned from the depth within, and I was sure she could be heard all the way down the mountain. No words, just the sound of a broken soul.

They scattered the ashes and I waited behind the tree. It was then that I heard it. I thought at first that a hiker had stumbled onto us and I was going to head him off and explain. It turned out to be a doe, a mother deer. Behind her came a buck with giant antlers. The doe, anticipating danger, twitched her ears and sensing none, stepped closer. I signaled to Jeff and Mary and they came around the tree. There, from behind a group of pines, came a baby fawn still wobbly on its legs.

A sign! The three of us knew it and we didn't utter a sound. The doe came up next to Mary and then sauntered away peacefully and effortlessly. The buck and the fawn followed and were gone as quickly as they had come. Without saying a word, the three of us started down the mountain. We knew we had seen a sign of life in the midst of death; that there were, indeed, many kinds of being in our Father's house and they all spoke of life. Becky would be all right.

We reached the foot of Tamalpais and it was Jeff's turn to cry. It was Mary's turn to be strong and supportive. How often I have seen a couple take turns breaking down and building up.

We drove across the Golden Gate and headed towards the airport. We hugged and said goodbye, knowing our lives would never again be the same because of Becky. And knowing, too, that the grief process had just begun.

CHAPTER 2

On Letting Go and Going on

To everything there is a season, and a time to every purpose under heaven: A time to be born, and a time to die; A time to plant, and a time to pull up that which is planted; A time to kill, and a time to heal; A time to break down, and a time to build up; A time to weep, and a time to laugh; A time to mourn, and a time to dance.

Ecclesiastes 3: 1-4

THE GRIEF PROCESS has a rhythm all its own. Like the seasons of the year, there is a winter of our personal lives, a time when we feel fallow and cold within, and a springtime of deep joy. This joy is no silly feeling, but rather a quiet urge which keeps on promising us that life shall come again. Even before a single leaf bursts forth on a barren maple, that tree is filled with life-giving juices pushing and surging upwards and out into the branches until the tiny bud becomes larger and larger, fat with the promise of new life. Just so in our human nature. Even as the winter wears on we can—at the same time—feel the advent of spring. We do not experience one season without the hope of the other. Indeed, good grief allows for both.

When does anyone face the fact that death has occurred? I have seen families accept it months before the death itself, and I have seen people who could not come to it for months afterward. Obviously, the manner of death is a crucial factor. Slow death gives warning. Sudden death gives none.

Funerals or memorial services are important. They mark the time when we officially recognize the occurrence of death. Without being maudlin, they may dignify tears which bring suppressed sorrow into the open. A mother must finally accept the fact that her child is dead. Avoiding funerals will not make the pain less, but rather will serve to lengthen the time of denial. The time faced, the place marked, we begin the rhythm of grief.

It's no accident that the process is often called "the management of grief." Given the proper framework and surroundings, given the strength of supportive family and friends, grief *can* be managed. We are not its victims. The journey is an adventure where sorrows once again lead toward sunshine, and sunlight dispels the shadow of The Valley. This is not to say that the journey is ever complete. Memories are forever. Scars will remain. But their outlines fade and heal with time and clear thinking.

When any soul comes face to face with the scheme of the universe, a dialogue is inescapable. Anger and tears, a feeling of uselessness and helplessness, and finally there is the acceptance and the interaction with the forces of life and death. Death is, and because this is so, grief must also be.

It begins with emancipation. That's just a fancy word for *letting go* of the power of death over us. It's a time to let go of the physical presence of the one who has died. It does not mean forgetting the past or blocking the memory, but it does mean letting go of the physical reality of his or her life.

How long does this first stage take? How long before we are truly able to let go? How long does it take to be emancipated from the physical reality of the one who has died? Every case is unique. Every person will adjust and let go at his or her own pace. The important point is natural timing, beginning the rhythm of grief, of holding on and letting go.

I remember a gentle older woman saying to me, "I lost my husband three months ago and every night I still sleep with my arms around his pillow. How long will it take for me to let go?" There's a natural answer. "Hold onto that pillow," I said, "just as long as you need to, and not another night longer. The time will come when you will be able to let go, but don't force the time. It will come when you're ready for it." She needed to know that she was experiencing a normal reaction to the loss of a lover, the desire to hang on just a little while longer.

Many people find themselves unable to leave the house after the grief process has begun. Often the home represents the final place of warm memories and every room resounds with the presence of the one who died. Pictures are everywhere but these can only be put away in one's own time. When the natural rhythm has worked its wondrous powers in the soul, one is finally able to leave the house and to let go even of the greatest of reminders.

One woman was offered a winter's flight to Florida the week following her husband's death. She told her hosts she was afraid the water pipes in her house might freeze while she was away, or something happen to the boiler. But the hosts were not to be dissuaded. She phoned my office and I gave her a blunt answer. "Tell them you're not ready to let go of the house yet, with all its memories, but when that time comes, you'll be glad to join them for a vacation." This she did, and her friends understood completely. It's much better to speak the truth about one's feelings in grief. Give friends a chance to understand and support you.

As soon as I returned from California, I talked with a young widow whose husband and only child, a son, went flying in a private plane to do some weekend fishing. Their plane crashed in the mountains of Vermont. Knowing that Regis had come through the grief process successfully and managed it nobly, I asked her to write down some of her experiences in a letter to Jeff and Mary. They were at a loss as to how to begin to grieve. This she did and beautifully:

Dear Mary and Jeff:

I'm sure peace is a very elusive thing with you just now. My first holidays—what a laugh to call them that—were a private hell. My friends and family were wonderful. I think I felt then that they were a little too solicitous; too obvious in their determination to be gay and cheerful in spite of "our" loss. They were trying in their way to show me that you "can't live in the past"—"life must go on"—etc. But, I also observed: they sat a little longer and a little quieter and held their loved ones a little closer than usual.

Be patient with your friends. There is no way for them to imagine the pain you are feeling. Most people think of death and all its aspects only when it touches them personally. How can they look in your eyes or listen to you and still pretend it can't happen to them!

I learned quickly which people were strong enough to accept me as a heart-broken, grieving person. I could draw strength from them. Others, I found, needed me to be strong. They could draw strength from me. Both were, and still are, very necessary in my life.

I thought about Michael, my son, and missed him more than Bob. That was a very hard thing for me to face for a long time without a terrible sense of guilt. I loved Bob very much and we had a very happy marriage. I hoped to grow gracefully old with him, but as in any marriage, there is from the beginning a thought that you might not—hence life insurance, estate planning, etc. Not so with Michael. He was forever!

For a while, I felt about them as though they were in an earthly situation. Bob was capable of taking care of himself. He was used to meeting new people. He would be brave. He would miss me, but he could understand and make the best of the situation. Michael was young. For all his seeming sophistication at an early age, he was still so vulnerable. He would be frightened. He would be lonely. He would miss me and be just old enough (and tall enough) not to admit he didn't understand. He would not ask for help!

These thoughts haunted me in the beginning— despite the fact that God had assured me they were all right.

I was alone at the airport. The plane was five hours overdue. My heart, my mind, my body gave in to the black hell of realization of what had happened. As I walked to my car, I heard someone screaming. I remember vividly the pain that was ripping me. I couldn't see. I was an insane human being. Then I was calm! I didn't see anyone; I was not touched, but I was calm. A thought was planted in my mind—"They are all right and you are going to be all right."

I thought then that it meant they were alive. When,

three days later, the plane was found with no sur-vivors, I didn't understand—but that thought was firmly planted. Even in all my sorrow, it repeatedly came to my mind and with it a beautiful calm feeling. I came to realize God had felt my desperation that evening and had assured me again of the wonderful truth of Eternal Life. "They were all right" didn't mean they were alive, but that they were all right in another Realm of Being.

This didn't keep me from missing them or having the thoughts I described to you earlier. It didn't take the pain away. As you observed, it never completely goes. It does become bearable—a part of you—a sort of strength upon which to draw. It has given every-thing in my life a deeper meaning.

Mary, I have tried to be honest. There were times I wanted to die. I repeatedly asked God why He took the two people in the world who knew how to live—who loved life more than any I have ever known. I was a bystander in the threesome. I partook of their adven-turous spirits, their desire to kick over every stone, to fly from a precipice, to build a bridge, to grow a rose. He never told me. He never told me because *He didn't take them, He received them when they came.* And I know Bob, Michael and Becky are all right whatever the Realm where they are now living.

Love,
Regis

Mary wrote back that it was exactly what they needed to hear. They had been unable to let go of Becky's physical presence. They clung to her as a baby in need of her mother. Mary worried constantly for fear Becky wasn't being cared for. Who would hold her in the night when she cried, and who would help her to walk? How would she stay warm and could she possibly be happy without her mother and father? All these fears and questions are based on the supposition that Becky is still alive as a physical being. A baby, lost somewhere, floating in space and wanting her mother. The letter from Regis set them free of this obsession. They began to let go.

Her letter makes a dramatic point, too, about the differences in emancipation. Regis tells how she felt one way in the loss of her husband and quite another in the death of her son. Had young Michael been an identical twin, and both had perished, it is safe to assume she would have further missed both boys in two totally different ways. Any parent of twins knows how different they are, and so how differently they would be missed. The same uniqueness of emancipation holds true when parents together grieve the loss of a single child. They knew him differently and they will each experience his death differently. The same child, but two completely separate losses. Each must be fair as he or she works through the pain of letting go, understanding that the other parent (or any other relative) must travel the road at such a pace and in such a manner as to be right for his or her unique personality and relationship. Each must find his own way home.

Tod's father said the reality of Tod's death did not hit him until two weeks after the memorial service. He had gone into the store in New York where he had always taken his son to buy clothes, and the store manager came over in his usual friendly manner. "Oh, Mr. Dodson," he said, "Where's your boy today?" The father had such a lump in his throat he was unable to answer. It was then that he faced it for the first time. There were to be other times, over and

over again, but the first one hurt the most. He knew he had
to let go, and in a fashion all his own.

I stayed with another family as they went through the
time of emancipation. For each, the process began differently.
Bob James died of cancer over a three-year period of
time. He had been a senior at Duke University when he first
noticed the lumps. An All-Conference soccer player and a
Regents Scholar, he still managed to deny the visible facts
until they could no longer be avoided. He underwent the
first of many operations and the beginning of the end.

The following year he married and began a successful
career with a large corporation. I asked them before the
wedding if they had any fears that this disease would return
and they said, "None at all." They were young and in love
and reality was a long way away. Officiating at the wedding, I heard them say their vows to each other and watched
them kneel and pray the prayer of St. Francis. When they
came to the end of the prayer, Bob put his head on Ellin's
shoulder. "For it is in giving that we receive, it is in pardon-
ing that we are pardoned, and it is in dying that we are born
to eternal life."

They went from strength to strength as his condition
worsened. At the hour of his death, the surgeon wept. The
staff left the room so that the family could spend time with
the body alone. Memorial Sloan-Kettering Hospital in New
York allows the family time to be alone with the body, and
this is most helpful therapy. It allows them the time to
adjust and to accept the fact of death. His wife, his mother
and father, brother and sister, all sat and held him in silence
for the hour.

But their reactions began to change. The widow and
mother were able to let go after the hour. They had no more
need to see the body. His sister agreed and went home in

silence. But Bob's father and brother had to be with him longer.

We made the arrangements for cremation but somehow the father was still not satisfied. The next day he drove to the crematory and requested the officials there to open the box before cremation. He needed one last look, needed to know his son was all right, and as long as his body was still physical, that he was at peace. Satisfied now, he let go of the physical reality of Bob and cremation took place.

Why was it so important for the father to hang on and not so for the mother or wife? These last two had come to accept his death before the event happened, and they needed no prolonged reminder of it. His father, on the other hand, had intellectually realized he was losing his son but viscerally he had not come to grips with it. Thus, he had to have more time with the body. It was also an unspoken need on his part to see Bob to the end. It was the task of the father to stay with his son and handle affairs at the last. To his mind, it was his natural privilege and duty.

Emancipation takes different forms and different amounts of time for each individual. My own feelings were so heavily invested in Bob that I could not bring myself to accept his death, either. I wanted to offer strength to the family I had come to love so long and well, but I found myself overwhelmed with grief for all of them—and missing their oldest son. It was hard to minister through those days.

But there had to be relief, too. When the room becomes heavy with memories, there is a need to rejoice in the good life shared. In this case, the church had organized a food caravan and different families brought dinner each night. Bob's sister turned to her surviving brother one evening and said, "It seems to me we ought to have some say in this. Call the church and tell them we want caviar and champagne tomorrow night. Enough of these casseroles!" It was what everyone needed. A time to laugh, and this we did with gusto.

The memorial service was attended by several hundred people. It was the public's time to assemble and declare the truth. They, too, needed to mark the time and place and so begin the grief process. The altar was bare, except for six wild iris on the table between two candles. One flower for each member of the family circle, including Bob. It was early evening and a spotlight picked up the intense blue of the iris. Because we had come to give each other strength it was not a sad occasion. I drew from them and they from me. We sang the great hymns of the faith, like "A Mighty Fortress is Our God." As I preached, Bob's wife kept encouraging me with a smile and a whisper: "Go on, you can do it." And I did. We all did together.

— IN MEMORIAM —
Robert G. James, Jr.

I want to strike a bargain with you before we begin these remarks. If for some reason I don't happen to get through them, or my emotions start betraying me—well, if you won't be embarrassed for me, I promise not to be embarrassed for me, either. A man should never be ashamed of his feelings.

I want those of you who were his friends through school to realize that Bob's last few months were quite naturally private ones. It's a time for deep thinking and quiet days, a time when energies are needed for survival itself. You can take great satisfaction in knowing that you helped fill those days with many laughs and good memories, the stuff of which real friendships are made. You made it possible for him to know enormous contentment these last few weeks and months, and so you have reason to rejoice.

It's true to say, I think, that if there is any weeping today, it's not so much out of sadness but more out of pride. We grieve much because we have lost much. I'm proud of this guy and what he has gone through these last years. He found value and meaning in his life, in spite of his circumstances, and so in this hour I hope you and I can set out to claim some of the things which Bob has already claimed and called good.

We can think of all that he discovered and silently told us. For one thing, he discovered that a man is not measured so much by his physical prowess as by how much he can endure, and how well he can endure it. Bob was known for his strength as an All-Conference athlete at Duke, but he was never so strong as when he was physically weakened by cancer. The greatest battle of his life was the battle for his spirit these last few years—and Bob won that battle. He discovered the infinite capacity of the human soul to deal with pain and disappointment and to come back, time and again, a stronger man of stronger spirit.

Then, too, I think he found the meaning of courage. Anyone can take up the future when most things are known and predictable, but to take it up when nothing is known and everything seems ominous requires courage of the highest degree. It's not a courage measured by brute force, but rather by a quiet confidence within.

He discovered that a man can survive pain as long as he feels he has a purpose through it. Bob found that purpose in his marriage and in his career, and both enabled him to keep going when others would have given up in depression. We watched patients around him die in the state of depression, because they had lost their will to live. Bob never lost that will because he never lost his purpose in living. That's a tribute to his marriage which gave him a reason to be, and to his business associates who kept him feeling valuable long after he could work.

There is no use holding back on it: Bob was in a great deal of pain these last few weeks, but what I would have us see is that he endured it with grace and strength—with a quiet gentleness that can only come from one who is well loved and comforted.

I have been thinking about how much he contributed to medical science. This is something which makes all of us enormously proud. He volunteered to be used for research in areas which did not even pertain to his type of cancer. You might call it a part of his plan. He wanted to make the best use of the worst situation, and he consciously gave of himself at every point. You should know that he had the best doctors and the best institutions that money can buy—the National Cancer Institute, in Washington, D.C., and the Memorial Sloan-Kettering Hospital in New York City—literally working with him. Those experts met their match in Bob James, and they admitted it. To quote one of them from a few weeks ago: "Frankly, he has embarrassed all of us. We left the ground of medical science over a year ago, and since then we've been groping in the dark. We do not know why he is still alive," the doctor said, "except for his diligence and determination. It's nothing we have done."

Finally, the doctors had no more experiments, and there were no more drugs to test—and Bob kept going. When he died last Thursday, one of his doctors wept. He had lost more than a patient; he had lost a friend. Said the doctor, "He inspired us to do more than we've done for other patients." He did not demand it, but rather he inspired it.

Someday, and maybe someday soon, they will find a cure for cancer, and when they do, we will, all of us, owe a great debt to this one who gave himself to that day.

Beside the research itself, I keep thinking what an inspiration he was to the other patients and to their families and to the rest of us. He found something to laugh about, even on the worst days, and he had a way of getting others to laugh, too. This is a disease that threatens to take away every thread of dignity, but Bob kept his dignity until the end. He knew what things he could manage to do and so with grace and a sense of purpose, he got them done. I remember one day, after he had been confined to his bed as too weak to walk, this guy talked us into loading him into a wheelchair, and with machines and bottles and tubes trailing behind him, he wheeled around the hospital. He simply refused to give up and that, my friends, is the mark of more than courage—it's the mark of human dignity. And he kept it to the end.

I think he knew he was inspiring others. But I don't think he knew how far flung are the results of what he accomplished. It goes beyond the circle of lives in this room today. It crosses all the lines and boundaries of age, and economics, and geography. Sick and well, rich and poor, old and young, all of us have been touched by Bob. He did not live in vain.

I've been thinking what kind of things he left to us all, what makes up his legacy. For one thing, he leaves us an example of what a human life can be. He taught us to look for the best of life in the worst of circumstances. He proved to us that every human being can be the exception to the rule if he tries, if he has the will to overcome. He taught us that cancer may kill the body, but no disease can destroy the soul. He taught us that so long as a man has courage for another day, he can find a victory at the close of that day.

Think of what he has left to our children, too. You know, when Bob was a child of five he hated pain so much that the doctors and nurses had to hold him down to give him an injection. The older he grew the more he learned about pain, until finally he turned and taught us all something about it. I think he would say to our young people that regardless of the insurmountable odds in front of you, regardless of how much things hurt sometimes, you can overcome it all with grace, and strength, and faith.

To these children he would teach living illustrations of those old Bible stories. He showed us a young man who felled a mighty Goliath called Cancer with nothing but a slingshot of faith and courage. He showed us living proof of three young men who were cast into the burning, fiery furnace of death—and escaped without a hair on their heads being singed. He showed us what the Bible means when it says that "Perfect love believes all things, hopes all things, endures all things." The Bible never said that love changes things—but more importantly, that it endures all things. And he showed us what is meant by perfect love casting out fear, for Bob was not afraid to take on anything—not even death.

To all of us, adults and children, he left a legacy of gentleness and compassion. I think if he were here today, he would express it something like this: "Speak a kind word to someone near you. Even if you must speak it through pain and sickness, speak it again and again. It will not make the suffering less, but it's bound to help heal the spirit. Take the time to thank the people who are trying to make life more comfortable for you. They're doing the best they know how, and they ask nothing in return. Don't be critical of people—life is too short for such as that. Don't sit in judgment on another person's life. In the long run, people tend to do the best they can with what they have to work with. Keep a sense of humor about things—laughter is good for the soul. And whatsoever things are true, noble and of good report, think on these things."

I tell you that's the kind of thing he would say to us, on leaving, because that's the way he lived his life as long as he had a breath left in him. These are a few of the things he discovered, I think, and a few of the things to which he contributed with his life, and a few of the things he left us all.

If I could have a final word, it would be one of thanksgiving. I think I speak for all of us here when I thank his family and his wife for sharing Bob with us.

Thank you for bringing him into this world and for bringing him up to be the kind of man he was. He always and everywhere gave his best. The six wild irises on the altar today represent a family circle which will never be broken. Not even death can break the power of love. You stood by him in beautiful and pure love all these years, being careful never to take away his dignity and to help give his life a sense of real purpose. No husband or son could ask for more from his family than that. And just so, God does not ask for more from any of his children than Bob gave Him. I believe he was one of the most magnificent examples of a human life I have ever known. I shall miss him. I shall never forget him.

Amen.

"Good night, sweet prince, and flights of angels sing thee to thy rest."

CHAPTER 3

A New Place to Stand

BOB'S FATHER INSISTED that we dig the grave ourselves. It was his last act as a father and, I think, he considered it his solemn and ancient responsibility. Contrary to America's modern way of burial, this seemed natural and right, therapeutic and healthy. It was a personal involvement in the things at the last. The family and I went alone to the cemetery with flowering dogwood and the wild iris, shovels and rakes and grass seed. We took turns digging and planting flowers and then we returned home to an empty house. It was time to face the new world.

New? Yes, and strange. This child they had conceived and brought up to be a man, this one who made life worth living, was gone. Nothing would ever be the same again.

The journey into this new world can be less abrupt if we go gently and thoughtfully. It is a critical point in the grief process. Things have been irrevocably changed, and we cannot deny it, but some things remain changeless. There are other children, perhaps, who need love and attention now, and the bond between mother and father, while shaken and tried, may be stronger. This is a necessary support system for any human being, that close relationships remain constant and strong when all else has been forever changed.

There are hundreds of letters and gifts to be acknowledged, jobs to be done which keep the mind and spirit active even when the temptation is to give in to despair. These social obligations can keep a family going for several weeks. The danger is that this activity might become a way of prolonging the first part of the grief process. It may become an attempt to deny the reality of death because it allows the living to feel needed by, closer to, the dead. In actuality, it should be seen for what it is—a means of expressing appreciation for the caring of others. I have seen families stretch this social period out for months until it became increasingly clear that they were using it in a negative, rather than a positive, way.

Entry into the new world is the second phase of healing. Each member of the family is drifting into his or her own new world. Each must face it alone and make of it what he can, supported by the family, but alone nonetheless. Since no one has ever loved exactly like any other, we must each grieve in our own way and in our own time. "Laugh and the world laughs with you, weep and you weep alone," becomes literally true. It's a new world. And a lonely one.

This is the time when the loss must be put into words as much as possible, when memory fights to recall and talk about the one who is missing. I say "fight" because in our culture it is just that. People in general do not like to speak of, or hear of, the dead. Neighbors and friends, even relatives, have a way of sweeping painful yesterdays under the rug. "Don't think about yesterday, just think about the future." This is small consolation for someone who needs desperately to remember. Just at the time when you most need to laugh and cry over memories, those surrounding you begin to treat the dead as a ghost, never to be brought into daylight again.

Jeff and Mary were exasperated because they couldn't talk about Becky without everyone else showing discomfort. Bob's wife, Ellin, went into a lonely shell because she sensed her peer group could not deal with open and healthy grief. Where once conversation had been spontaneous and bright, now it was filled with avoidance. This was a new world.

If you are fortunate enough to find a select few who will listen, seize them! Take them into your confidence. You will soon learn who it is that will strengthen and support you, and who it is that you must strengthen instead. You will sense the difference immediately. The latter want to believe that you're made of strong stuff, that you can keep a "stiff upper lip" and that you're so independent you need no one to tell your feelings to. They're reflecting their own weakness, not yours.

Speak of him. Speak of him again. If a certain phrase reminds you of yesterday, then say it: "That sounds like something Bob would have said!" If clothing or colors or favorite activities remind you of the past, say so. "Bob loved crossword puzzles. The two of you could have had a great time of it. He could come up with the wildest words."

People are sometimes afraid to talk about the dead because they fear their own deaths, and also because they are afraid such words might make the grieving person more unhappy. So it's up to you to set the stage for good grief here. Tell them you are not disturbed and, in fact, you want to remember. They will never know unless you tell them. They will never relax unless you help them.

There's a very good reason why you will relish this conversation of memories. It assures you he is not forgotten; that his life was not in vain.

Tears from the depths begin about here. Especially if the death was a sudden one. These are not tears of shock and dismay. These are tears of the soul. It's all right to cry. It's even helpful. Cry out of bitterness, cry out of a sense of loss, cry just because it feels good to cry. But for God's sake, cry. It's a part of being human. Be proud of your tears—you grieve much because you lost much. The love was real.

In the middle of sparkling conversation, I have seen people break down and cry. Their tears were brought on by laughter and good times, memories of the way it used to be, when suddenly something was triggered in the depths of the heart. Grief is letting go of anything which used to be a precious part of us, and this means we are going to let go slowly and with a great cutting of the soul.

The shortest and most revealing verse in the Bible refers to tears. "Jesus wept." When he lost a good friend, Jesus wept. How much more God expects us to weep when we have lost a lifetime! A child grew up and died before he had a chance to really live. This is worthy of heartfelt emotion. All that you are has been invested in one who is dead, and you have a right to cry. So go ahead.

Your new world is a strange land. Just as life around you is not the same, you will discover a depth in yourself and in your values which you never before realized. Only one who has truly suffered can know the depths of the human soul. Bob's mother, Ardis, remarks now that she has learned more about herself and her relationship with her God than she ever before appreciated. She's quick to say that she'd gladly trade it all to have her son back again. But that's not one of her choices. And it's not one of yours. So take advantage of the pain. Don't become its victim. Learn from it, grow with it, deepen and mature. But never fail to rejoice in

what you discover in the new world. You cannot raise the
dead, but you *can* increase life.

It's reality therapy in a way. Regardless of what friends
and relatives say, tomorrow will not be like yesterday and
the one who sorrows best realizes it most.

But never be afraid, either, to hope in the midst of your
tears. No one will come along to replace him, but there will
surely be others who demand your affection and your love.
They need you to reinvest yourself again, to take up life
again. You have an even higher sense of the living experience
now, so plunge into your new world with hope and faith.
It's true that you must journey there alone, but bear in
mind that you're not the first to go there. The widowed and
childless who have gone before you can testify that this new
place of being can be a place of beauty and deep peace.
Yours can be the grand task and joy of claiming these days
and calling them good. Nothing will ever again be quite the
same, yet still there is more life to be found in your new
world. And that life can still be good.

CHAPTER 4

Reinvesting Yourself

STRANGE THAT IT SHOULD HAPPEN NOW, just as I write this chapter. I buried Bud Cremin today. For seven years he wanted to die, prayed to die, tried to die. But there was just enough will to live that he lived on in spite of himself. In hell.

Bud saw his new world after his wife died. He had a couple of lunches with friends. He tried a job. He even went to see a physician to try to determine the reason for his lethargy. But nothing beyond himself could snap him out of it. He simply saw the new world and didn't want it. Mentally, physically, and spiritually he decided to begin to die. This morning I said the last benediction over his life.

Just seeing the new world is not enough. You must decide to reinvest yourself in that world, to find new meaning and to grasp new reason for being. It sounds so easy. Often when I lose one I love in my work, I go through the same stage. I've looked out the window and not given a damn that the sun was shining or that a black squirrel was making a rare appearance up in my oak tree. Conversations seemed frivolous and senseless because the great purpose in my life was gone. Oh, I knew that I would reinvest myself, but just then I didn't want to.

Bud never did. He practically stopped eating, except when neighbors came in with stacks of TV dinners and outlined his eating routine for the next several days. This they did because he infrequently allowed visitors in the door, and never when they brought something they had lovingly prepared. It was more than he could bear. He stopped coming out of his house a couple of years ago, except for midnight trips to the mailbox on the corner.

Some time after I had buried his wife, I dropped in on Bud to talk some serious sense into him. He knew I didn't really understand. He knew it from the beginning. Once in the door he made the welcoming remark, "If I had known it was you, I wouldn't have let you in."

"Are you eating any better these days?" I began. "No." "Do you have any desire to go out for lunch with some friends who'd like to see you?" "No." "Bud, tell me the truth. Do you care if you live or die?"

"Yes. I want to die."

"Well," I said as I took his hand, "If you ever decide you want to live, call me. We want to help. But there's nothing anyone can do until you make that decision." I suppose I was trying to shock sense into him. I wanted him to understand the gravity of what he was allowing to happen to him. No one was doing it to him. He was allowing it to happen to himself. He was choosing.

In the Bible, it was Isaiah who first coined the term "broken hearted," and that was the malaise of which Bud died. That, plus a heavy overdose of self-pity. The neighbors found him on the floor, his dream completed, his ultimate wish fulfilled.

Bud was an extreme example of what happens to all of us

when we take a look at the new world and can't quite decide to give ourselves to it. Most people can cross over the border and take up some form of life again. Bud never did.

I remember one woman coming to me a few months after her husband's death and saying, "I wish to hell they'd buried me along with Earl." I knew she was half ironic, half serious. She meant it, but she didn't mean it. She was caught between the two worlds. It was time for a decision and just then she wasn't sure she could vote in the affirmative. "Alice," I said, "You're too mean to die. Besides, who'll be around to run my life? And who'll be around to be grandmother to those children? What you're feeling is perfectly normal, so don't feel guilty about it. But don't let yourself believe that you're actually going to follow through on it, because you won't."

"What makes you so sure?"

"I know you. You want to stick around long enough to see how the whole thing turns out!"

Another woman came crying that the new world would never be the same as the old one. Of course it wouldn't. But it could still offer a whole new quality which she had never before seen. Everyone's life has some bad with the good, and now it would be her task to sift through both and start seeking more of the good. Somehow, and only she could answer how, she found it.

"They say that time heals all things," she came in later to say. "Well, I'm here to tell you that it doesn't. I still hurt. I still miss him and cry for him. But I'm finding things I enjoy doing and I'm doing them. I found out right away that I'd never fill the rest of my life playing bridge with the girls. That lasted about a week. Then I stumbled on child care, living with children while their parents are away. When they return, I have my freedom back and my days to myself, and then I can accept another job when I need it and want it."

That discovery might not work for everybody. But each of us has a new discovery to make. Yours will be uniquely your own and it will only come when you take a cold look at the new world and decide to reinvest yourself in it.

I'm thinking of the woman who called me one night in deep depression. "If I should not be here one of these days," she said, "I only ask you to understand. I have the courage to go on living, but I don't have the purpose. I've seen enough of this life without him and I can't bear it any longer."

In this case, I knew she was serious. I went to her and cried with her, worked through options of new living, but nothing looked appealing to her. To this day she has not found it, but I'm convinced she will. She has financial security and now she knows that this alone offers nothing. It will be up to her—no, deep within her—to find the purpose in living again.

Suicide is such a normal reaction at this stage. Don't feel guilty about it. Everything worth living for is gone. But do something positive about it. Find new things worth living for. Force yourself to get out of bed in the morning.

Get out of bed. That, again, sounds easy to people who've never been there. But if you can just put one foot in front of the other, you'll make it. And if you can convince yourself that you're making it, you'll keep on making it.

Don't wallow in self-pity. Don't give your darkest memories and saddest hours prime time. When the shadows overtake you, bolt for the sunshine before it's too late. Concentrate on what a friend is saying to you. It's not frivolous, it's a part of life being shared with you. Seize it. Try to get into it. You will make it.

A part of me rejoices that Bud got his wish. But another part is sad tonight. If only he had wanted to reinvest himself, he could have made it. I just know he could have made it.

The old Biblical truth comes home again: "They were lovely and pleasant in their lives, and in their deaths they were not divided." He wanted it that way.

CHAPTER 5

Signs

IT'S NATURAL TO SEE SIGNS and hear voices. Don't feel crazy, but be a little careful how you interpret them. Some people hang on to these signs as living proof that the one who died is still very near, physically. They want to believe that he or she is communicating with them from the other world and that our two worlds are very close together.

A more healthy reading of signs is to see them as *reminders* that the love which was will always be. It's only normal that a life which has had such an impact on your own will be strongly felt after you are physically separated. There is a tie like the phenomenal tie between a mother and her new-born baby. No one can quite explain it to everyone else's satisfaction. So we stop trying.

Just so with signs after death. The tie that binds is real and it's bound to show itself in beautiful and touching ways. The door to the basement he always left open is open again. No, he did not open it (perhaps you left it open), but it can be a quiet reminder of the way he used to do things. Or didn't do them.

There are other kinds of signs which need to be taken seriously, signs of hope and comfort when everything is dark. Could these be a gift to us, just after the death event, from the Creator of life, Who wills that we sustain ourselves and take heart?

Like the day we scattered Becky's ashes on the mountain. The little family of deer that came to stand with us were no figment of our imaginations. They were a sign, that family of three, to the sorrowing mother and father. Becky would be all right.

When Regis heard the voice that calmed her, following her husband's and son's deaths, it was very real to her. It kept her sane, enabled her to get in her car and drive safely home, and it comforted her through the despair of indescribable loss. Losing all she had in this world might well have destroyed her mind. But the voice kept softening the hurt, promising her that they would be all right.

We quickly learn when not to talk about the signs. Practically everyone thinks we are either lying or crazy. Who ever heard of such a thing? That's a normal reaction—for someone who has never needed eternal hope, or even mortal reassurance. People often tell me of the signs they saw, the voices they heard, following the death of one they loved. And I believe them. Yet together we agree that not many people would understand and so we keep these miracles our secret. We tell no one.

There comes a time, however, to stop looking for signs. The grieving one who saw a rainbow just at the darkest hour need not keep looking for rainbows forever. They simply won't be there. No, rather they come just when the storm is past and we are in need of a promise. And then as mysteriously as they come, they go.

I can think of no better illustration than Don. He was such an amazing character that he left an indelible impres-

sion on all of us. Polly, his wife, kept seeing signs after his
death, and so did a lot of us. He touched us that deeply.
Our souls kept reaching out for his.

Don was, at one and the same time, an alcoholic, a math-
ematician, a scientist, a dedicated jogger, a spinner of tall
tales, a corporate executive, a philosopher, humorist, and
friend to all. He precisely marked down every lap he jogged
and at exactly what time he would run into the house again.
He charted every cigarette he rolled and allowed himself
exactly ten a day. No more. No less. He was forever educat-
ing people, even when they didn't want to be educated, and
teaching them the history of this ethnic group or that
heritage.

He was a true Scotsman who wore his Cameron tartan to
parties and always raised the question as to whether or not
he had anything on under it. He never stopped talking, and
if he did someone was sure to beg him to start again. He was
that funny, that interesting, that wonderful.

Three days before Thanksgiving, he left on his daily jog
with his usual comment to Polly. "Bride, I shall return in 47
minutes, God willing."

He didn't return. Some strangers found him behind a
tree. He had had a fatal heart attack. Behind that same tree
he used to stash bottles of booze (and behind a lot of other
trees, too). He even hid them in old tires in the basement
and behind cereal boxes. Polly always found them but Don
was determined. Regardless of the public's misconception,
alcoholics are determined people.

Joining Alcoholics Anonymous arrested his disease, but it
never changed his nature. He still got into Polly's side of the
bed first and warmed up the sheets, and then slid over to his
own side so they'd both be warm. He still counted every

minute as a treasure, was quick to use his binoculars to spot wildlife, and loved to tell you the time of day the sun would set. To the minute.

Every community, every synagogue, and every church needs some reminder of redemption like Don Hough. He picked people up when no one believed in them and he brought them back to sanity and sobriety. If ever you dropped in at his pre-Revolutionary War house, he would fix you a drink because he firmly believed alcoholism was a disease of chemistry, not character. But whether you wanted whiskey or cranberry juice, his message was the same—just take it one day at a time and love every minute of it.

We had vacationed together on Nantucket island a few months earlier where he regaled everyone with stories, led us across the sand dunes, and announced the moment when the seagulls would land. They landed as announced. He was so alive, so sensitive to the universe, so beautifully in touch with the earth that for the first time in my ministry, I could not accept a death. Don couldn't die. But now I know he did.

I packed my toothbrush and shaving gear and moved into the house. Two groups began descending on the place and it was a cross section of true community. Alcoholics Anonymous and the Church. Everyone had stories to tell, moments about which to laugh, and laugh we did. Hundreds of people brought food and drink and faith into that shocked household. Polly and the girls kept pointing out the fact that Don had just graduated the week before—his oil portrait had been elevated from the bedroom to the living room. He had made it.

The recovered alcoholics told stories of his coming to them in the middle of the night, cleaning their houses when

they were too drunk to remain healthy, and even mopping
their kitchens. And then taking them off to dry out somewhere. When no one else believed in their right to life, Don
did.

The family and I sat down to write the worship service
which was to be held on the eve of Thanksgiving. It was not
a funeral but rather a memorial service. We had a great deal
for which to be thankful. Of course, we had to have a
Scottish bagpiper and the tunes of Scotland. One of the
daughters wrote the statement on behalf of the family;
another daughter played the traditional parting hymn on the
flute—"You'll Take The High Road and I'll Take the Low
Road, and I'll Be in Scotland Before Ye"—and the youngest
wrote the benediction.

The great swell of the organ broke through the soft
candlelight that night and the packed sanctuary was overcome with the vibrancy of joyful love. We sang "Come, Ye
Thankful People, Come," and we meant it. Then, alcoholics and staid churchmen alike stood together and sang
"Blest Be the Tie that Binds." We knew we had all been
bound together, not just by Don, but by what he taught us;
that if we help each other, care for one another, we'll somehow make it together. We were singing the ancient message
which so many of us had missed.

The bagpiper, wearing the Cameron tartan, began in the
front of the church, in the chancel, and piped "Amazing
Grace" down the center aisle and out into the hills. It's the
Scottish tradition. Finally, all was silent.

Then the statement from the family:

I am the youngest of the Donald Houghs, and together
we wrote a message dedicated to him. Daddy struggled
and puzzled but always kept on running. He reached a

peace, a perfect peace of understanding, full giving and forgiving. He gave us his love of life. He gave us his life of love. And so, on behalf of the family, his "bride of these many years," Paulina; Cammy, "the eldest and fairest"; Tina, "the Swedish one with the big wide smile"; and Connie, "the little one," we would like to give back to him all the joy he gave to us. Please rejoice with us in the knowledge that Daddy, the Old Master, has finally solved all his equations, is now in a new dimension, and as he would say, "Top Notch, Never Better."

— IN MEMORIAM —
Donald Hough

I smiled this morning at the thought that if only I could preach the way Don Hough could tell stories, we'd be here all night, and we'd be laughing ourselves into the morning. And we'd be loving every minute of it. Fortunately, Don is not writing his own eulogy, so we can all expect to be home before midnight.

Here it is the Eve of Thanksgiving, and there could be no more appropriate time and way of commemorating Don's life. His family, his friends, and all of us gathered here in this church are filled with hearts of love, pressed down and running over with thanksgiving that Don Hough touched our lives. Maybe that's the problem. It feels so good it hurts. It's so absolutely overwhelming and glorious that we keep crying out of gladness. How strange, some would say but I say how natural! How natural to cry from the depths of our souls in ecstatic happiness and thanksgiving, because it's here, in the depths of our souls, where Don broke through to us.

I'm thankful that he showed me the heights to which a human being can rise. He proved to all of us that a man can pick himself up when he's down and lift himself up to the heights of being fully and beautifully human. He was a man like few I have ever known, and I loved him for what he was and what he became. Personally, I was always so proud of him that I wanted to show him off to all my friends. I wanted to say, "Look what Don is today and look what he's made of himself!" I wanted to say, "Now that's my idea of a true man of God." I wanted to say, "You and I can do that, too, if only we tap the source of his faith and take up his courage and strength." I guess what I'm saying is that I not only loved him, but I loved loving him. You felt that way, too. He made us proud of him, yes, and he also made us proud to be human.

Then, too, I'm thankful that he died at the high tide of life, rather than in the ebb of it. How wonderful it is to leave when the party is in full swing. How terrible it is to hang on too long, weary and broken, when life has ceased to offer richness and the personal touch of love. No institutions for Don. No paralyzed years of frustration and sickness. I'm rejoicing tonight that, for Don, life was always an experience in the good. Life was a process of climbing higher and higher . . . one day at a time.

I'm thankful that he exemplified the best in being a father. He told us, through his life, that he treasured most in this world his "three presumed daughters." He never asked them to be any more than they could become, and he guided them every step of the way in becoming just that. They put the gleam in his eyes which told all of us where his earthly treasure was, and where his heart was also.

I'm thankful that he showed me the best in being a faithful husband. Most of us have heard him tell those wild and embarrassing stories about Polly, and when we looked closely into his glistening eyes, we knew he was speaking out of silent reverence and respect and deep, deep love. His was a quick and brilliant mind, tuned to the precise and scientific. But always and everywhere his highest and best thoughts were of his marriage and the one who stood by him through life. What a love story between two lovely people. Together, they gave us a glimpse of heaven on earth. They taught us the meaning of the Divine relationship, of faithfulness and eternal love. I cannot think of Don without thinking at the same time of his family. I cannot think of what he made of his life without thinking of the people who helped make it possible. And so, I think, it shall always be. They are inextricably bound together, and no power on earth, not even death, can break their bond of love. That calls for a little rejoicing!

And now, to the family I say . . . We know his story could have turned out a different way. But you four would not have it so. Hang on to what you gave him. Treasure it as he treasured it. No husband or father could ask for more than Don received from you. You have filled our Thanksgiving this year with a special measure of Divine gladness. Tomorrow, as we gather together around our tables, we will hold each other a little longer, and we will hug each other a little more closely. We will be enormously thankful, not because we're suddenly aware that we might lose someone some day, but rather because you've made us aware of what a blessing it is to love someone today—and to have someone love us. You've taught us to be thankful for that.

I shall always remember him for the witty ways, too. I liked the way he used to answer the phone when people called, and he always said something like, "Don't despair! The check is in the mail!" And now what I hear him saying is simply, "Don't despair. I'm all right." And remember those times we would phone for one of his daughters, and he would say, "Is Connie here? Well, she's not *all* here, but you can speak to what's left of her."

Let me conclude by speaking directly to two groups of people. To those of you who shared his church and shared his life as neighbors and personal friends, I say, take inspiration from this man. He inspired us to be our brother's keeper. He taught us the meaning of good neighbors. He showed us the value in looking always for the good, the true, the pure, and the beautiful, and thinking only on these things. He brought out the best in life, so take inspiration from him. Let me tell you a little story to bring it home. While most of us have been stopping by to visit Polly and the girls these last few days, Polly sneaked away yesterday to visit a grand old Scots woman in the hospital. In her thick burr she told Polly a story about Don. She said she remembers him best the day he came to call on her when she was sick at home. He had never met her, but he heard she loved Scotland, and so he arrived at the door all sunshine and smiles, in full tartan dress, carrying the flag that says, "Scotland Forever." That was Don. His brother's keeper, his sister's friend. The Good Samaritan. The love of Christ made present in our lives. Polly says we made a church-man out of Don. I say he made Christians out of us.

Now, to those of you here who shared the fellowship of AA with Don, let me tell you that we, too, honor and respect your loss of a comrade. We have no secrets here, so let it be shouted from the skies that Don gave dignity and holiness to your cause. In fact, Don got me so excited about AA one night that the two of us decided to write a sermon on the parallels between the Church of Christ and Alcoholics Anonymous. We came to the conclusion that you have a truer church on earth than most churches we know.

We did not know it then, but how prophetic were the words he helped preach that day. Let me quote him: "It's never considered a battle won and done, but rather a continuous race that is never finished until this life is over." Listen to this, and let none of us forget it. Don finished his race a sober man, a man of dignity and courage and deep faith. Take inspiration from him. To those of you who were sponsored by Don and pigeoned right up to the end, I want to say for him, "Don't give up!" Draw strength from the same power from which Don drew it. Call it a higher power, or call it what you will, but Don called it God, and he was never ashamed to name Him as the source of his strength. I think Don is saying to each of us, and all of us, regardless of the individual battles we face, ''Just take it one day at a time, and keep the faith.''

Let's hear again the words of Paul we have selected and put them in new perspective: '' . . . The time of my departure has come. I have fought the good fight, I have finished the race, I have kept the faith. Henceforth there is laid up for me the crown of heaven . . .''

Well, Don must be enjoying this to the hilt. We're sending him off in the style of a true Scotsman. With bagpipes and candlelight, laughter and tears, friendship and love, we've come to blast the heavens with our own version of a twenty-one gun salute. ''Top notch. Never better.''

So let there be much rejoicing in our thanksgiving. Let us praise God for the life of a noble and good man. Let there be much hope in our grieving, and let it be the hope of Heaven itself. Let us take up the good fight, and finish the race, and let us keep the faith—as Don kept it—one day at a time.

Amen.

''Goodbye, you who made me. Smile a mile and glitter and glo.

Love, your girls''

It's no wonder Polly saw signs. A lot of us saw them. When the skies were cloudy, she glanced down into a mud puddle and saw the reflection of the sun. A sign? Perhaps, but most important of all, a reminder. When she needed to see a rainbow, she saw one. When she needed a glimmer of hope, he came to her in some miraculous form and reassured her.

Are some of these signs simply of the mind? Or just

conjured up from memory of what life was like when that one was with us? Or are they gifts from God to comfort us in our deepest hurt? I don't know. It seems to me none of us will ever know. Rather, we should simply take them as they come and give a little thanks that a shaft of light breaks through the shadows.

Time will come when the signs must depart. But that will be a natural time. No need to force it. For now, hold tight to the memories and the hope. Don't feel crazy. Feel warm and close and thankful.

CHAPTER 6

Not Guilty!

GUILT USUALLY RUNS RAMPANT through all the stages of grief. This is the time when you suffer a severe case of the "If onlys." "If only I hadn't said that, if only I had done this." But now it's too late.

Love at times demands a certain assertiveness of will and discipline. Polly felt guilty when Don died because she remembered the day when she came home and found he had drunk a half bottle of whiskey at ten in the morning. She quickly uncapped the bottle and poured the other half over his head. "There," she said, "This one's on you. Isn't it fun?" Later, she regretted it. But that morning she did what love demanded.

Those things happen. We do what we must because at the time it seems in the best interest of our relationship, or at least of the other person. Nina felt guilty because she spoke harshly to her husband just before he died. He was told not to exert himself physically, but he was chopping wood when he dropped dead of heart failure. Nina didn't want him out there in the freezing weather, working so hard. But that's exactly where he wanted to be and what he wanted to do. She yelled at him to get inside the house before he killed himself, and those were her last words to her husband.

Out of love she did what was in the best interest of his health. She was right in what she did, but of course she felt guilty. Then she felt guilty because she wasn't standing beside him when he died. "If he was going to make a fool of himself, I should have gone out there and stood beside him." But that runs contrary to trying to bring him back into the warm house. Guilt following a death seldom makes good sense.

People want to know they are loved when they die, but they do not want their last moment to be ugly to those they love. Nina's husband would have wanted to experience his final heart attack alone, with dignity and privacy. We don't want to burden those who love us with a memory they will never be free from. We'd rather go peacefully, quietly, and then be found by someone who cares. Bill was like that. Nina had no reason for guilt, but still she felt it. Her vow was to stand next to him "until death do us part," and Nina is the sort of woman who wanted to be faithful to those words. So she felt guilty.

Jeff and Mary thought of all the times they'd disciplined little Becky. But what child doesn't need firm guidance? All of us feel bad for the things we said and did when the recipient of our words and actions is forever gone. We feel guilty, not so much because what we did was wrong, but rather because what we did cannot be undone. Ever.

But what of those words that were indeed harshly spoken and without love? It's only fair to say that every love relationship has within it moments like these. And it's also true to say that, deep down, the lover understands.

There are so many kinds of guilt to be felt and remembered. Most of them need to be blocked until you can cope with them and then let go in due course and with strength. But most of them had a reason, at the time, and if they didn't have much reason, they were at least secretly under-stood as part of the relationship between two people.

I remember one woman who caused a great many people to feel guilty after her demise. Gert Batten was one of the most eccentric characters I've ever known. She seldom said a kind word about anyone or anything and delighted in mak-ing your day miserable. At least it seemed that way. She lived alone in the old house her father had built and left to her, and she hadn't changed a thing. The poor old woman still cooked on a wood stove and maintained the decrepit place just as her father left it. She was nearly 80.

Some of the neighbors felt sorry for her, but most of them wouldn't go near her. You could find her almost any day out in the garden, wearing coveralls and an old white shirt, tilling the soil and pruning the trees. The garden was her life. She didn't like to dress up in lady's clothing or play sophisticated games. She was plain-spoken and earthy in her ways. In the midst of an affluent community, she still had an old water pump in her front yard which needed priming, and the house hadn't been painted since her papa died years before.

Neighborhood kids played baseball on the property adja-cent to hers, and when their balls landed in her garden or yard, she raced to retrieve them and stashed them in her cellar. That would teach them. Miss Batten was the meanest woman they had ever encountered. She stole their baseballs.

I knew another side of her. She followed the progress of those children and, when there wasn't enough money, she came to me with a check for their college education. But the guarantee was that I would never let them know it. If the family wanted to write a letter of gratitude to the benefac-tor, it had to be sent to the church and I would re-address the envelope and send it along to Gert. But they were never to know. And they still don't.

She delighted in being difficult. Downright mean is often a better term for it. When friends dropped by with homemade bread and soup, she often reached through a hole in the screen but would never open the door. They went away ungreeted and unsung. They didn't understand that Gert loved their kindnesses but didn't know how to receive them formally or thank them.

Gert was only comfortable with a few people, but she was careful not to let them know it. They drove her on shopping junkets and delivered supplies when she was too ill to leave the house, but still she seldom invited them in for coffee or friendship.

Their feelings were not always kind towards Gert, and they were to grow less kind as the days wore on. One old friend received word from her doctor that she was to stop chauffeuring Gert around town on shopping sprees because her blood pressure was showing signs of aggravation. Gert could do that to people. But the friend continued to help, nonetheless.

Gert insisted on being driven across town to save three cents on a can of soup, and then back across town to save a nickel on a giant box of soap. Never mind the wasted gasoline, just save that penny! Gert saved every one of them.

Shortly before she died, Gert called me to say they had taken her wood stove away and replaced it with a piece of modern junk. She was in deep depression. Everything from her childhood, the mainstay of the old house, had been ripped away. She was sure she was about to die and even more afraid that she would be carried off to a nursing home.

"Gert," I said, "I'll make you a promise. As long as you

can take care of yourself and live in that house, we'll see to it that no one takes you away. You stay healthy to the end, and I promise you we'll carry you out of that house feet first." There was a long and happy pause on the other end of the phone. Suddenly she was living again. "Okay! That's a deal."

One Friday afternoon a friend from the church went by to leave milk on the back porch. She knocked on the door and there was no answer. Something told her all was not well in the homestead. She called another friend and the two of them carried Gert out of her old house—feet first. She lived long enough to bid farewell to her most valued friend. "Goodbye, house," she said, "Goodbye."

The penuriousness ran in the family. When I called the only living relative, a distant cousin in another state, to tell her the news, she had only one question: "Who's paying for this call?"

Neighbors felt guilty. Friends felt guilty. Church people felt guilty. I felt guilty. What more could we have done to help that woman enjoy life? There was so little for her that surely we could have increased the good. What did we say wrong that made her so unhappy and difficult to be with? And most of all, we felt guilty because deep down we simply didn't know how to love Gert.

As one friend of 30 years put it, "I feel guilty for not liking her. I waited on her hand and foot for years and never once did she repay my efforts or even say thank you. I can't help but resent her, and I feel guilty now that she's dead."

Another old friend called with a confession. "Since you're my minister, I have to tell you something. I just discovered I'm not a good Christian. All the things I did for Gert don't mean a damn thing because I never enjoyed doing them. I did them because they had to be done and someone had to take care of her. But my heart was never in the right place."

"You're the best kind of Christian of all," I said. "Even though you got knocked down at every point, you kept trying to make her happy. Even though she was mean to you, you kept trying to be good to her. Don't give me this unchristian stuff. Yours is the living faith because it's been filled with good works, in spite of your heart. You have no need for guilt. You should be enjoying the fact that you were faithful to her, even when she didn't know how to express her gratitude."

The phone kept ringing. It was obvious that guilt and misunderstanding were running loose through the community. "Why such a wasted life? Why so much bitterness and unhappiness? What did she want us to do? What *more* could we have done?"

I called the funeral director and arranged to have her buried in her old coveralls and white shirt. I was half afraid the good Lord wouldn't recognize her if she came through in a dress. Besides, the gardens of paradise might need a little work.

We arranged the memorial service for Sunday noon, immediately following the worship hour. I wanted as many people there as possible, to help them understand the other side of Gert and to relieve them of their guilt and bad feelings. It was obvious that they wouldn't have made the effort to come out on another day. So we arranged for a captive audience.

— IN MEMORIAM —
Gertrude Batten

Some of us wanted to select a hymn to be played today which would symbolize the unique and earth-touched life of Gert Batten. It will be played softly and we will sing it quietly because Gert didn't like loud music. She always said that was the reason she didn't come to church. It was only one of them. Her church was in her garden, and, because she lived alone, we have selected the old hymn, "I Come to the Garden Alone."

When Miss Batten spoke, she was always direct, concise and to the point. It seems to me our service in her memory should be the same.

I simply want to say that she was one of the most unique and unusual human beings I have ever known. I often thought that if the church did not have a Gert Batten, we would have to invent one. We would need to know of someone who stood up for her rights, who was outspoken at every point and was not afraid of man or beast. We would need in our lives a reminder that the frills of life are not important, that life is centered in the earth and anyone who lives next to the earth has little time for small talk or gaudy tinsel. She was cantankerous and wonderful, both at the same time, and you know, I think she thoroughly enjoyed being Gert Batten. Even when she was angry with me, that gleam in her eyes told me she was savoring every minute of it. Because she knew I secretly enjoyed it, too. I just want to say that I think she had a good time being our Miss Batten.

How thankful we can be that she lived the way she wanted to. No system or bureaucracy was going to get her down. If the city government told her she couldn't burn her trash, she went ahead and did it anyway. It was her house, and before her it was her father's house, and no bunch of young upstarts was going to tell her what to do. She lived life her way.

How she loved that old house, the home of her family for whom she never stopped grieving. How she loved cooking on that old wood-burning stove. My only regret is that she outlived her stove because she didn't want to. She liked life in the old manner, not expressed in fancy new appliances. She knew the value of the dollar, but that wasn't enough. She even knew the value of the penny! Her only complaint was that the rest of the world didn't know its value or appreciate the way it should be spent. I want to say that Miss Batten wasn't so much close with the penny as she was wise in her spending. She didn't enjoy the things from which other people derive pleasure.

So what did she enjoy? I think she enjoyed her friendships. Miss Batten didn't need a lot of foolish words to tell people how she appreciated the way they took care of her and visited with her. She just assumed that if you were a friend of hers, you understood that she was a friend of yours, too. To you who cared about her, worried about her and looked in on her for so many years, let me say that her childlike eyes gave her away—she loved every one of you, and she was grateful for your caring.

She enjoyed children, too. The gifts she gave to others will always be held in confidence, but I think she would not mind if I told you that she gave of her resources to educate and clothe children who had real needs. As the Bible says, she did not sound her trumpet on the street corner for all to hear of her goodness, but rather she gave privately and quietly. How she loved to show children around her homestead. She showed them through the barns and the smokehouse, and she took them around the property pointing out every tulip tree and evergreen and azalea. In her own way, she knew she was showing them a world they had never seen before, and they would never see again. She gave that gift to our children.

And she enjoyed her garden. It was so much like a family to her. She worried over the trees and fretted about the blight taking over the horse chestnut. She was so proud when the creeping myrtle came out in full blue and beautiful bloom, and she knew joy when the lily of the valley resurrected for another year. I don't know what will happen to that old and gnarled wisteria tree that wound its way around her porch railing and into her soul, but I thank God it was there all her life, and that it gave her so much pleasure.

There are no children to grieve for her, but I'm convinced her spirit knows that her garden will miss her very much. So shall we all. It was the garden, I think, which kept her in touch with God. There she saw death turn into life, winter give way to spring, and the rebirth of the spirit was ever within her.

There is a story which comes to my mind today. It says a lot about the kindness and goodness that was within the heart of Miss Batten. It's about an Englishwoman who appeared before the gates of heaven and knew she was due entry there. St. Peter looked under "Elizabeth Jones" and could find no record of her life on earth. "Tell me something you did on earth," he said, "which should open the gates of heaven for you."

"Well, I was chairman of the Altar Guild of the Church of England for twenty-five years. That should count for something up here."

Seeing how smug the woman was about that, St. Peter said, "I've looked under Great Church people and there's nothing there with your name on it. Besides, that really doesn't count for much in heaven."

The woman thought a while and then she said, "Look under Generosity. I gave large sums of money away and surely that should get me through the gates."

St. Peter looked under Generosity and then under Big Spenders, and he found nothing. "I'm sorry," he finally said, "But there's nothing in the Book of Life which makes mention of any of your great acts."

The woman turned to walk away, and suddenly a thought occurred to the gatekeeper. "Wait a minute," he said, "would you by any chance be the Elizabeth Jones who used to feed the sparrows in Piccadilly Circus?"

"Well," she said, "I did enjoy going there and feeding the birds, but surely that's not enough to please the Almighty."

With that the gates swung open wide and St. Peter went rushing out to embrace the old woman. "Don't you remember," he cried, "that God cares for the littlest sparrow that falls? The Almighty has been waiting for you, just for you, to say 'thank you' for feeding his birds, for taking care of the least of these, for of such is the kingdom of God."

That was the Miss Batten we knew. She tended her garden and fed the littlest sparrows that fell to the earth.

Let me close with the way in which Miss Batten's life closed. A short time ago, we made her a promise that as long as she could take care of herself, her church would see to it that she could stay in the family homestead to the last day of her life. We would carry her out feet first. So many of you worked to keep that promise. You took food to her, shopped for her medicine, and looked in on her every day.

How beautifully it all ended. An institution could possibly have prolonged her life, but that would have been no life for Miss Batten. Friday afternoon, two old friends came calling on her and, with help, carried her out of that house—feet first. She was a wise woman, in touch with the earth, and she knew what was about to happen. But she also knew a promise had been kept, and her friends had been faithful to her. Could anyone ask for more than that? She lived life her way, and she died her way. So we have no cause for grief or guilt, but only for thanksgiving.

I've even been spiritually smiling to myself all weekend. It seems to me that heaven is going to be in for a workover. If anything is not perfect, though I suspect most things are, Miss Batten will have it taken care of or know the reason why! She'll make heaven a better home for all of us.

And I'm thankful too, just now, that the God who walked in the garden with her can now welcome her home at last. Perhaps just now he needs someone to feed the sparrows; perhaps just now

he's even rejoicing that someone has come into the Kingdom to take care of the gardens of paradise. I think she'll like that.
Amen.

> For, lo, the winter is past,
> the rain is over and gone;
> the flowers appear on the earth;
> the time of singing is come,
> and the voice of the turtledove
> is heard in our land.

People were soon to discover they had no reason to feel guilty about the poor life of Miss Batten. When the attorney and friends went to clean up the old house, they found a few surprises.

The furniture was a shambles. Torn and sagging. One woman turned a chair over to see if it could be rebuilt or salvaged, and she found a few hundred dollars stuffed in the springs. There was more in the sofa. When they reached to take down the curtains, they found hundreds more rolled up and stashed in the curtain rods. And it's no wonder the piano was out of tune. Gert had stuck cash between all the wires. In the breadbox was an extremely valuable coin collection. Tucked in her stockings and clothing was a fortune in coins and cash.

No wonder she didn't want people coming in her house. It was her bank. At least it was one of them.

When the will was probated, there were even more surprises. Gert left several thousand dollars to the friends and neighbors who took care of her through the years. It was her way of saying "Thank You." She left money to the church, to a relative, and hundreds of thousands of dollars to children's organizations and national charity groups.

The neighbors had no reason to feel guilt that Gert lived in such humble circumstances. She wanted it that way. She enjoyed priming the pump and cooking on her wood stove. Even old friends began to understand that her lifestyle was her choice, that she relished blunt words and hoarding her pennies.

They're tearing down the old house now. The garden and grounds are being subdivided into several housing lots. It's called progress. The proceeds will go into her estate which is still being counted and distributed across the country.

They're finding her odd collections. She loved to collect things. Horse shoes, garden hoes, weed hooks from days gone by. The old barns are filled with yesterday.

And who knows? When they finally dig up the cellar of the old house, they just might find the world's largest collection of baseballs.

CHAPTER 7

The Anger of It All

SOMETIMES IT'S HARD to distinguish between guilt and anger. What feels like guilt may well be anger which needs to be expressed and dissolved. At other times, when you feel angry, you're only feeling guilty that you didn't do more.

Every death brings with it some portion of anger, but not all people will express their anger in the same way or at the same objects. Some see the medical staff as being incompetent and uncaring. Others blame God. Others lash out at the neighbors or friends or clergy who didn't do enough, didn't come around when they were wanted and needed.

I know of people who have carried anger concerning another's death for years, and to this day have not expressed it. It remains bottled up inside and manifests itself only in destructive forms. Like getting angry at little things which have nothing to do with the real object of pain. Or turning to the bottle, or withdrawing into a narrow world where no one can cause disappointment again.

When you lose someone you truly love, it's only natural to be angry. Especially if that someone was vital and young and full of life. It just can't end all of a sudden without someone, somewhere, giving a decent explanation, or at

least attending to the last moments with extreme understanding and care. So you get angry. The problem is not so
much anger, but rather how you choose to vent that anger.

Some people suppress it and feel guilty. "He died so
unhappy that it must be my fault. I didn't know what to
do." They are angry with themselves. This is anger at its
most dangerous level because it has nowhere to go. It lives
buried deep as a boiling pit of lava and every so often it
erupts in all the wrong places.

One man came to me, having lost his father, and he was
truly furious at his wife for not allowing him to love his
father during the years of their marriage. Of course his wife
allowed it, but it was his own choice not to make more visits
and pay more attention. He had a demanding, domineering
father, and the truth is there was not enough attention on
earth to satisfy that old man. The son was left feeling the
brunt of it all, and it turned into anger against his innocent
spouse. What he had chosen to do was love his wife, tend to
his children, and call upon his aging and ill father as often as
he could. He knew this was not enough to placate the old
man, but it was all he had to offer. What he did was right at
the time, but what he chose to feel afterward was guilt—and
it surfaced as anger at his poor wife.

How much better it would have been to be able to say,
"I'm angry that nothing I ever did satisfied my father. He
demanded more of me than I had to give. It was his nature,
and I understand, but it wasn't fair to me or my own family." That's placing the anger where it belongs.

I recall a young woman who was angry with the doctor
because he never told her the serious facts of her husband's
case. The truth was that the doctor tried to tell her, but she
refused to listen. Rather than cope with the guilt of not
facing reality and cherishing those last moments together,

she turned in anger on the physician. "Why didn't he come right out and say it?" she asked me, "Rather than disguise the truth. I would have quit my job and stayed home to take care of him."

That is misplaced anger. It would be better to feel the guilt and realize that at the time she simply couldn't quit the job because they needed the income, and she didn't *want* to hear what the doctor was trying to tell her. If she could do this, then she could see her anger as guilt and forgive herself.

Conversely, I know of a family who took out their anger on just about everyone who came their way. They became more than strict parents to their other children after their infant son died. They turned tyrannical, so outraged were they at their loss. The autopsy showed that the child died of an incurable disease, and their physician knew and never told them. They had every right to be furious with the doctor, but because they are of the firm belief that doctors can do no wrong, they took it out on their children. And anyone else who came along.

We're trained not to show anger in our culture. It's not polite. It's not pleasant. So we bottle it up, and let it loose in the most untoward places. How much better to see reality for what it is, to get angry in the right places, and thus vent or dissolve that anger just as surely as a blood clot is dissolved. Both can be lethal if not properly treated. It's no use pretending that we're not angry if we are. In spite of our training not to show it, we feel it. And the only way to remove it is to work on it, talk about it, properly place it, annihilate it, even if that involves driving into the country and crying and screaming.

If it's a question of anger at a particular human being, there is a question of forgiving that person, once the harm is established and understood. If it's a question of anger at ourselves, then it's a matter of forgiving ourselves and knowing that we are indeed forgiven.

Of all the deaths I've encountered, most of them among the young, not one of them has conjured up anger like Tod's. We were contemporaries and I loved him as a friend. His was a terminal heart condition at twenty-four, which meant he moved too damned slowly for most of us. He didn't need to be hospitalized, just cared for and understood. There were times when I couldn't understand. Life moves too quickly, and I felt I couldn't miss a beat of it.

He had one of the finest physicians I've ever known. His family was well aware of the short life span he had left, and so was he, and so were we all. But he lived on and on. Sympathy wore out, and friendship wore thin. The undercurrent was something like, "Either get well and get with it, or go to bed and let us feel sorry for you." But Tod wouldn't do either. He just kept plodding along.

Patience, that's what he had, even with his own dying. Few of the rest of us had it. In time he began to look like living death, his eyes jaundiced, his skin blue from lack of circulation. No one wanted him around at social gatherings and even fewer wanted to stop in and ruin a pleasant afternoon.

He volunteered at the hospital one hour a day and he volunteered at the church an hour on Sunday afternoons. He was only good for that hour each day.

Behind the scenes, his parents were working to give him energy. They dressed him and carried him down from upstairs, so that he would have the strength to leave the house and contribute something to life. He was barely able to get one foot in front of the other, but somehow he kept doing it. Would this guy never wear out? Never.

I was angry that neighbors didn't do more, and angry

that church people didn't stop in more often. His peer group abandoned him, and those who stood by him often did so because he gave them instant purpose. They would be gone in a matter of days.

I was angry with myself because I didn't want to be with him more. We used to enjoy going to the doctor's office and getting his blood count every week. If the count of white blood cells was above a certain level, lunch would be on me. If it fell below, he paid. But the joke turned sour, and I wanted out. His mother was left to take charge of him, and for this she needed no help. But, as a young man, he needed mine. There were days when I just couldn't give it to him. The clock was moving, and I couldn't wait forever for him to revive or retreat. Limbo was the worst of all.

One night, in his living room, he told me he thought he was about to die. At that point I didn't want to hear it. Pain that he was to me, I loved him. "You're not going to die now so let's change the subject."

I was not about to give him up. A part of me didn't want to hang on, and another part refused to let go. I didn't like hearing him talk about the truth we both had to face.

"I want to die with my boots on, man. Then I want to give my eyes to two teenagers, and I want to give my heart to medical science so they know what this disease can do to a young and good body."

And the cross around his neck, he said, would be mine. When he had his heart attacks, his body would shake as though it were the end of life, and always Tod would grab that cross and hang onto it. "I get this lump in my throat and I get scared, and all of a sudden I hear this voice inside of me saying, 'You'll be all right, man, calm down. I'll live with you, I'll die with you, and I'll take care of you no matter what.' And you know what? The lump in my throat, it just goes away."

The next morning his father drove him to his volunteer job at the hospital. The phone on his desk rang and when he reached for it, he had his last heart attack. It was so massive and quick that he never knew it. He was wearing a pair of cowboy boots at the time, so at least he got his last wish: He died with his boots on.

I was angry with myself and others at first, and then I realized that a lot of the anger was just misplaced guilt. I would have to forgive myself and come to realize that friendship demands what we give it, and when we have given it, there is no need to feel guilt over not having given more.

The anger I felt at others would have to be realized for what it was, and then I would have to honestly forgive them. They did not mean to abuse him or abandon him, but he was too much a reminder of what must some day happen to us all. And besides, Tod was slow and life moves at a fast clip. I could not change the scheme of things, but the least I could do was forgive those who were caught up in it. I had been there, too.

The anger and guilt would have to be worked through and dissipated before the memorial service. I knew I would either break down in tears of remorse or lash out in vengeance if I did not satisfy the inner feelings. And forgive.

All the afternoon of the service I kept trying to write the words of tribute for that night.

There was only a single red rose opening on the altar. It was from his family.

— IN MEMORIAM —
Tod Dodson

Tod Dodson lived his life as a gift—a gift from God to be given, in turn, to others. We use powerful and profound words when we speak of him as courageous and strong. These are good words and true, but I wish to speak for a few minutes (for him, and with him) about the source of his courage and strength.

Tod had what I can only call perfect faith. In that respect, he had an advantage over most of us. He had been given, years ago, good reason to consider closely the meaning and the purpose of existence. Rather than measure life in years, he measured it in substance. And that substance, for Tod, was faith. Perhaps in this hour we will discover something about his faith and leave this church ourselves strengthened and of good courage.

Tod's faith was not an escape; it was for him an affirming truth which led him through every day. He was not afraid of life, and he was never afraid of death. Last week he put it this way: "Why do you think people are so afraid of dying?" I said it must be because we haven't thought about it enough, at which Tod laughed and said, "Man, you don't have to think about it; you just have to trust God." There's more truth in that statement than 2,000 years of theological dissertations.

His gift was made greater, too, because of hope. Perfect hope. Where you and I are inclined to measure hope in terms of longevity, or success, or good health, Tod measured it in terms of eternal hope. He was never afraid that a new job, increased activity, or some long trip might jeopardize his chances for living longer. He was more concerned about his usefulness as a person, about fulfilling his purpose on earth, than stretching idle years into more idle years. It says a great deal about his character that Tod's last minutes were spent on the job, working for no money. We can all learn something from that kind of eternal hope which puts the values and cares of this world in a different perspective.

The last part of his gift I would mention is this: Perfect love. It's only natural that we ask ourselves, in retrospect, "What more could we have done." I ask myself that question and feel guilty knowing that I failed him in some ways, and then I remember something. Tod always knew that people tend to avoid unhappy situations, and there was never malice in his heart or anger because people stayed away. In his own words, he once said: "I know people are afraid. How can I let them know I understand?" That, my friends, is perfect love. Rather than feel guilty over what we did not do, let us receive more perfectly his gift of love: He forgave. He knew, and he understood.

Tod was supported by love. His life was rich and full. To his doctor he was more than a patient; he was a friend. Tod managed to get more mileage out of a trip to the doctor's office than seems possible. He never went as a sick patient but rather as a personal friend of practically everyone in the building.

He was surrounded by love. To his parents and sisters, I want to say that you can be enormously and forever proud of the home life you gave Tod. He asked for no miracles; he only wanted to be a regular son and a regular brother. He was that because you worked hard to make him that. He wanted his young manhood; he wanted his integrity as a human being and, because you allowed him to make his own decisions and assume responsibility for those decisions, you gave him that. He was fully aware of every sacrifice and effort you made for him. Treasure that family love which binds you all together, because it is real—and he treasured it.

His was a rare gift of life. I never knew him to speak an unkind word about any human being. He wasn't made that way. He never complained about being cheated, because he never measured life in years. He only asked to do the best he could with the years he had—and he did that. Those of us who loved him are not sorry for his life; we cannot be sorry for his death. But we will miss him.

Let me assure each of you in this room tonight of something very real. In the last few days it was evident by the things he said and did that Tod was feeling a very profound joy. He was feeling more complete and ready for perfection in the love of God. It was then that the great miracle of Tod's gift of life began to happen. A few nights ago we were laughing and talking about how good it was to be comforted by that voice within him saying, "everything is going to be all right." He made me promise then that if anything should happen to him, his death would be used by a team of famous heart surgeons to learn more about the disease. Because of his desire to make of his life a gift, people who suffer that illness will have their days made brighter. Beyond that, Monday afternoon in New York City, two young people who were blind were given Tod's eyes to see. That's a grand tribute to the man, and it is the essence of his religion. He received life from God and gave it willingly and unsparingly to others, confident through perfect faith, hope and love that his new life would be eternally perfect through Jesus Christ.

Tod would laugh about what I'm going to do tonight. There was a song which always started his every day and sent him on his way with joy. It was written by Charlie Pride—and even the thought of it makes me laugh. We liked to disagree about his taste in country-western music, and yet when it comes down to it I can resort to nothing better than these words to describe the meaning and purpose of his life. Tod was right: It's a great song in praise of God and His infinite caring.

> Let Him always walk beside me,
> Let Him take my hand and guide me;
> Let me live in the light of His love,
> Till I reach that great tomorrow,
> Where there'll be no pain and sorrow;
> Let me live in the light of His love.

> Let me live! Let me live! In the light God's love can give!
> Let it shine like the sun up above!

Let me feel every ray,
Every night and every day;
Let me live in the light of His love!

Let us vow that his gift shall not have been lived in vain. His was an excellent life, and there are so many things we can do to pass it on to others who desperately need his faith, his hope, and his love. For Tod's sake, let us begin now.

Amen.

"Walk and be not faint, friend. Run and be not weary. Then mount up with wings like eagles and be at peace with God."

CHAPTER 8

Postscript to Suicide

THE GRIEF WHICH FOLLOWS SUICIDE is filled with a horror unlike any other. Not only does it bring on the predictable feelings of shock, guilt, and anger, it also leaves one feeling a failure—rejected, despised, ashamed, embarrassed, and utterly humiliated. For many, suicide is the one great and unforgivable sin. It is the one act which God will not pardon. Until recent years, in fact, suicides were not allowed Christian burial in many churches. Punishment was hell and forever.

It is no wonder, considering this enormous social and religious stigma, that families often seek ways to conceal the act under another name. I am told by one official with the National Center for Health Statistics in Washington that every year there are some 28,000 recorded suicides in America. But, he admits, most suicides are not recorded. For reasons of insurance payments or personal honor, thousands more intentionally destroy themselves in automobile wrecks and household accidents each year. Then, too, out of deference to the survivors, coroners across the country will sometimes complete the death certificate by listing the cause as heart failure, unknown, or even natural.

In the last year alone I have been involved with three suicides both within and beyond our church membership. One young man drank poison which he found under the kitchen sink; a woman drank a lethal dose of alcohol; and a man took an overdose of pills. None of these was recorded as suicide. There was a bare thread to hang onto that "perhaps it was an accident." In each case, neighbors and friends—and even children within the immediate family—were not told the facts. But my experience has been that they all came to know the truth in time.

Both of my grandfathers took their lives, as did my gentle uncle last year. We've made it an unspoken rule in our family never to speak about the manner in which they died. Unfortunately, there is also the corresponding understanding that we cannot mention the way in which they lived. The final act has dimmed all the good which preceded it. But I do remember, when I was young, finding an old newspaper obituary which was well hidden in a relative's closet. My grandfather's name was in bold letters across the top and it was then I learned his first name. A fine name, I thought, a solid name. I remember thinking, "Here he is!" as if I had actually stumbled onto the missing man himself, and then being tremendously elated that I was finally in touch with the roots of my beginnings. Like so many items in local papers in those days, it was brief but exact. It said that "he came home last Sunday night from attending services at the Methodist Church and killed himself."

It was all I ever knew about him through my youth and I treasured it. I was so thrilled to learn that he was a "church goer" that I even forgave him for being a Methodist. (Gallows humor can be a saving grace for those of us who must endure the unspeakable.) Then, in my adult years, I began writing relatives and asking questions of my parents. I wanted to know how my grandfathers lived, not how they died. It was a source of belated pride to discover they were loving and serene men, devoted to their families. They were men of strong faith and deep conviction. They worked hard to provide for their children. One plowed the soil, the other worked in the city—but both lived close to the earth. They were humble and good men. Mine is now a new thanksgiving for my heritage, and especially for my grandfathers. I'm proud of the way they lived. I have come to accept their manner of death, and even the reasons for shrouding it in silence all these years.

It is of extreme importance in surviving the mystery of suicide that you not judge the thinking, the secret feelings, the fears, and motives that led to it. The rationale which culminated in death has absolutely no rhyme or reason to the outsider. You simply may not stand in judgment. The dark moods before the act itself can follow great victory or achievement, as well as crushing defeat. It's difficult for us to comprehend, but unusual and prolonged elation or manic happiness can be quickly followed by severe depression. It is a medically recognized fact that many new mothers experience something vaguely familiar to this after the birth of a child. Black moods are often fostered by some abnormal high. They can come like a streak of lightning out of the clearest blue sky. That is, there is no analyzing the particular or even the general kind of thinking that leads to voluntary death. However it felt to the one who suffered through it, however it came, you and I did not experience it and we can never fully understand. We heal more quickly if we cease trying. Of one thing you can be sure: no single event or problem brought it on so stop searching for a source of despair so critical it caused a man to take his life. If all the elements of coping with everyday stress are normal—mental, physical and spiritual—no outside occurrence can trigger a human being to kill himself. For the person feeling affirmation towards most of life around him, any single or even combination of problems only presents a choice of options as to the best solution. Such is clearly not the thinking process of those who commit suicide.

So we cannot judge. Consider for a moment those slow acts of suicide which are tolerated and even socially encouraged in our society. These happen every day and they are certainly not considered "sinful." There are around us constantly those people set on killing themselves by drinking too much, smoking too much, quietly overdosing on pills, blatantly stuffing themselves with food until they bloat and call for more. Every vital organ of the body is singularly and, sometimes, systematically destroyed—brain, heart, stomach, liver. The central nervous system goes haywire and the regenerative processes of the body can no longer repair the damage. If not direct, these are surely indirect methods to the same end. A conservative estimate of many hospital administrators is that at least forty percent of all admissions for illness and surgery are alcohol related—not counting auto accidents! This figure, of course, does not even attempt to include the admissions due to problems of abuse of tobacco, food, and drugs. Such habits can impair the mind until it does not think clearly or react quickly. The end result may be a household accident or a car wreck. To be sure, many people who overindulge do not consciously wish to harm themselves, but we can be equally persuaded that a considerable portion of them do. They are at least relatively conscious of the destructiveness of their actions. We rarely blame them for killing themselves slowly and publicly. We seldom label their destruction a sin. But, in the end, they are no less dead than those who choose quicker methods.

And what of those who lie in hospitals and nursing homes

crying out all day to die? Tied to bed rails or strapped in wheel chairs, foreign tubes snaked through their insides and plugged into computerized machines, I have heard them *pray* to die. I have heard them plot every conceivable means of killing themselves. Every week I used to go and visit a young friend of mine in a nursing home and try to communicate with him through the maze of tubing and machinery. His speech was barely audible and he could only beg me again and again to help him die. I used to pray for him to be attacked by a respiratory infection that would kill him. Two years later he died after months of being subhuman. So what of him and people like him whom we never see because they are kept away from the public eye? Shall the church call their prayers a sin? Shall we call their desperation to die wrong? No, we cannot. We simply cannot judge.

Just so with those who suddenly take their lives. Their minds experienced similar torment, at the end, and no one can understand how excruciating their vision of life had become. If we can forego blame and condemnation, a time of healing will come to our souls. We will be able to stand apart from the act itself and let God receive the one who goes out to Him with a disconsolate hurt too deep for mortal mind to comprehend.

You and I are helpless. We cannot prevent self-destruction. The postscript leaves us brooding about ourselves and our relationship with the suicide. During the first burst of grief, then, try to assert your power as a human being by thinking in new ways. Try to realize that there was nothing you could do before the fact and the very best thing you can do now is to suspend judgment, hold onto your affection and esteem for the dead person. Rid yourself of the feeling of rejection and unload your guilt. These are not simple for those of us who survive suicides, but they affirm the fact that we have not been stripped of our ability to think, act, and feel in ways which are constructive and conducive to new life.

That sense of having been rejected, for example, is hard to shed but it is essential if we are to put our lives back together. Whether it is the death of a spouse, parent, young person, sibling, or friend, we will naturally experience some feeling of rejection. The goal must be to rid ourselves of it. Carrying it around is a little like packing too much baggage for a short trip. The excess weight becomes a nagging burden that can spoil the whole journey.

You might begin unloading by remembering that he or she was not so much rejecting the loves of this life as hoping to find a new and more complete form of love in the life to come. For some people there is something womb-like and wonderful in the thought of death. It is a perfection of all that is imperfect, an event which translates all questions into answers and serves as the final soothing balm for the wounds of existence. In its own way, death is very like what the world was before we came into it. Here is the essential purity of creation.

Those who take their own lives are not so much concerned with hanging on as they are fascinated with *going* on. If holding onto this life offers no prospect of healing, going on to the next is at least a hope. Stewart Alsop, when he lingered toward the end of his life, wrote "There are times when I do not want to die, yet times when I do not want *not* to die, either. Death seems like my good Uncle Thanatos who will come for me and take me home."

When the cares of this world are no longer endurable, there is, for many, a strong attraction to what promises to be serenity in the world to come. How many of our gifted artists and poets have taken their lives, only to have their biographers unravel years of courtship of and fascination with death. Like Alsop, there were times when these sensitive souls did not want to die, and other times when they did not want *not* to, either.

The feeling of rejection in such instances brings with it extreme guilt. We feel guilty that the struggling person did not turn to us in the last great hour of need. "What kind of friend am I that he didn't turn to me?" It's another way of saying we think we were not worthy. In truth, he didn't turn to us because he *couldn't*. The "black dream" of the last and most severe stages of depression simply cannot be communicated to another human being. It can only be borne terribly and privately. And so he could not discuss with us the ultimate decision to end his life. Because it is not a rational decision, based on the same picture of reality as the rest of us see, the person contemplating suicide cannot possibly talk about it with a rational, realistic friend. Here is a "given" that no one else can understand. It is not a reflection on you personally or your relationship. Rather it is an unconscious decision about the way life appears to him.

Doubtless you have rehearsed in your mind what you would have said if only he had come to you. But even if he had, your words would have fallen on deaf ears. While private therapy and helping relationships offer affirmation and new options for those in the early stages of depression, even the best of psychiatrists cannot break through to anyone who has already decided to die. Often therapists go so far as to tell the patient that it is, indeed, his decision and they relinquish the power and the ability to keep him from changing his mind. The hope is, of course, that the patient will find a new vision of self once he is actually the sole arbiter, or that he will at least come to the edge and then realize that he is not truly serious about it.

I remember once working with a depressed man for many weeks and one day receiving a call from his psychiatrist. The physician urged me to stop trying to talk the man out of suicide and turn him loose to discover that he didn't really want to go through with it. Not long after that I had my chance. We were driving down a back road one rainy afternoon when the man asked me to let him out of the car so he could lie on the railroad track and kill himself. It is hard to recall any decision more difficult than that one, but I pulled the car over and told my friend goodbye. I can still picture my last sight of him as he plodded up the tracks in the rain, looking for the perfect place to end it all. He called me a few hours later and asked for a ride home.

But had that story turned out the other way, it would have had disastrous repercussions for everyone—patient, family, friends, physician, and minister. I'm certain that I would have spent the rest of my life feeling directly responsible. Yet he proved to all of us—and most importantly to himself—that he was not truly serious about his intentions. Today he is functioning quite normally and feels good about himself and the world around him.

Surely this story must cause us to wonder what spells the difference between my friend and a person who actually follows through on the threat. We like to think we can differentiate between potential suicide and the one who merely talks about it. In the end, we cannot. Both sorts travel the same road and leave the same troubling clues along the way, but one is asking for help and the other is announcing the end. We might approach both sorts with the very same kind of help but, for reasons unknown, only one will accept it. Nothing we say or do will dissuade the other from taking his life.

Some three months after my friend decided to walk away from the train tracks and phone for a lift home, a strange suicide occurred. A young woman who had received several years of private institutional care and been released as responsible came home to visit her family and then drove to the same crossing and threw herself in front of the next train out of New York. I'm certain that her psychiatrist and friends and family were no less supportive than his, but the blunt difference is that the young woman literally intended to kill herself and no power on earth could change her mind.

It is so with most people who finally take their lives. There is not enough we could have said, if called upon, to have altered their plans. They were incapable of hearing us.

Remember, too, that the external events and persons in the life of a would-be suicide can create confusion, frustration, and normal depression, elements which in themselves are simply not enough actually to cause self-destruction. If more people understood this, grief would not bring with it years of deep remorse. So, do not allow yourself to feel rejected or guilty. You were simply not that important to the final decision. It was a black dream more overwhelming than the reality of life. You did not cause the horror and neither could you cure it.

I perceive the mind just before suicide as being like a sophisticated piece of machinery that has shut down. When I think back to my childhood in the West, I can still hear the roar and whine of the gigantic food production plants my father used to own. Day and night these mills ground the grain and toasted it into bite-sized chunks of chow. The furnaces and engines were located miles from our house but I could hear their roar and whine every night when I went to sleep, and every morning when I woke up. Once in a long while the hubbub would cease. It seemed as though the whole world had stopped. Within minutes, engineers were climbing the ladders and inspecting the mechanical intricacies. As often as not there was some minor problem in

the wiring system, yet it was enough to kill the whole opera-
tion. A circuit overheated, perhaps, and the whole precise
machinery was reduced to absolute silence, all motion
paralyzed. Then the circuit was repaired and immediately
the furnace fired up and the engines began roaring and
whining again. Production resumed and once more life became normal.

It seems to me our minds are like that. For some, the
wiring can be repaired because the problem is found. For
others, repair work is not in the least helpful because the
problem cannot be located and the power is bound to blow.
Then the whole plant shuts down and production cannot be
resumed.

When such an event occurs in a family, there is good
reason why parents do not want to tell their children. In a
society where too many people still think of it as a conscious
decision equivalent to outright, unpardonable murder, they
do not wish the social stigma to be passed down another
generation. They have allowed themselves to be convinced
by church and society alike that because suicide must be a
crime, the perpetrator must be a criminal. And so the terrible ordeal is shut in the closet with the rest of the family
skeletons. But children have a way, when they are big
enough and curious enough, of opening doors. Sooner or
later, then, the truth will out.

Our concern must be not *whether* we should tell them, but
rather *what* we should tell them. To the very small, you can
speak in simple language which they can understand. If
they have questions about the specifics—and only if they
have questions—you can say that "Mother got very tired
and wanted to rest. It's like when you get tired of playing
and you want to come inside and do something quiet for a
change. She didn't want to leave you. In fact, she wanted

you to remember how much she loved you. And you'll always have that love tucked inside your heart." For those a little older you can talk in more mature terms. "Daddy wanted to feel completely good and not have to worry about things any more." About here you can remind them of the kind of symptoms he displayed before the final decision and how this was his way of healing those wounds. If he was physically ill, for example, then they will understand that he chose to be well again. They will no doubt gain enough knowledge with the passing years to question whether the decision was the best alternative, but at least the foundation for healthy acceptance has been established in the young mind. When it's of prime importance for children to carry respect for a parent, you will be helping them think of the deceased in positive ways, rather than carrying bitterness, anger, guilt or, worse—shame.

It matters most that you explain to the young that it was not a malicious decision *against* anyone. Neither was it a decision based on the normal problems children bring into a household. This relieves children of all ages from feeling guilty because they made too much noise around the house or caused too many problems for the parent to endure. You should talk about natural childhood and adolescent antics and let them know their behavior did not cause the real problem. They didn't do anything "wrong".

As the children mature, they are certain to encounter episodes of depression. It's natural for all of us to experience depression, but those of us who are related by blood to someone who committed suicide are going to be especially desperate at times like this. "Is it a sign of the end?" we wonder. "Will it continue to get worse? What will happen if I don't spin out of it in time?" You can be supportive by telling these young people that everyone gets depressed and, in fact, many people get severely depressed from time to time. For the most part, it's perfectly normal. Just as nature is a recurring rhythm of winter and spring, so human experience is one of fallow times and joy. The dead person's depression has nothing to do with his relation's present depression. We each live out our own battle of the night. We can each find our own way to the morning. No other person's action, even suicide, can dictate ours; a tendency to suicide is simply not hereditary. Adults old enough to understand, including people plagued with fear of taking the same step, should mark well the observation of the deeply spiritual physician Paul Tournier: "Fear creates the very thing it fears." This is our problem—that we might think ourselves, frighten ourselves, into the very thing we do not want to do. Let me put it another way. If we have an enemy in the suicide of a relative, it is not the act itself but only the *fear* of that act. This fear can balloon out of all proportion until we deceive ourselves into thinking we have inherited a sickness. We have not.

Regardless of who or what has gone before us on the stage of life, we are free, for the most part, to write our own scripts. True, the script for each will be written around certain opportunities or limitations, strokes of luck or bad breaks, and designed for the roles we are given—but we are still free to create our own script and to fashion our own ending. We may not be able to predict or control everything that will happen at the last, but we can at least choose what will *not* happen.

Ours is a God who makes all things new again, ever creating and recreating our lives when we have the need to forge into unknown territory. We journey there best when we walk one day at a time, not worrying about the future but letting each well-lived today take care of the morrow.

This is essentially what God was saying to the prophet, Elijah, when the loyal fighter slumped into the cave of depression. Elijah had just come down from a great victory and as he pondered the reality of his life he decided that he would rather be dead. "Take away my life, God, for I am not fit to live." But God loved Elijah and He willed another day for him. He understood the depression of the prophet but He also knew there were other options, at least for him, than death. He instructed the prophet to accept some bread and water, and so to fortify himself for the journey ahead . . . "Or else it will prove too great for you." How God understands the mind of severe depression! He did not ask of Elijah great things by and by, but only the motivation to sustain himself through today. Food, and then the promise of purpose which is the journey ahead. I think of all the characters God addressed through the Bible and always He knew precisely of what they were capable. He empowered Sampson to move the giant pillars, and he set free the entire nation of Israel from bondage in Egypt and led them towards the promised land. But for Elijah, these vast goals were not possible. God only asked him to take a little food and water and so sustain himself for the future. The ancients who wrote the poetry and stories of the Bible seemed to have an instinctive knowledge that our God is a personal and understanding God, expecting only as much as we are able to give.

It's interesting to note that suicide is never really judged in the Bible. It seems to be more of a value handed down from the organized church than the first peoples of God. Judas Iscariot, one story goes, went out and hanged himself. Nowhere do we find a value judgment on the act itself. We are supposed to learn from the lesson that once he betrayed Jesus his life lost all meaning and purpose, not that suicide *per se* is a sin. Warriors and kings of the Old Testament had a habit of falling on their swords or at least asking someone else to help them do so. Again, it was always because their minds were in agony or they had come to no good end—but their manner of death, as such, seems not to be the point.

Yet I firmly believe that God wills life for His children. He loves us with an everlasting love. This love is so personal, understanding, and all-knowing, that He must surely care at the heart for the person who cannot keep going. I am persuaded that God does not consider such suffering people as quitters or even sinners, but rather that He knows their innermost desires have stopped pulsating and their minds have shut down. What close communion there must be between that agonizing soul and the God who once Himself agonized on the cross. They, too, must feel betrayed as He felt betrayed, and the hope is that at the last they commend their spirits to Him. I suspect there is no closer moment between the Creator and His human creation than that moment when we finally let go of all the values of this world and hold only and forever to our God.

It's very like the mother of eight children who was asked if she had any favorites. "Favorites?" she replied, "Yes, I have favorites. I love the one who is sickest until he is well. I love the one who is in trouble until he is safe again. And I love the one who is farthest away until he comes home." If God is concerned for the one sheep which is lost, and we believe He is, then how much more concerned He must be for the one soul which is suffering beyond endurance. How He must long to come for him and take care of him. If God knows every hair on our heads and every sparrow that falls to the ground, and we believe He does, then how much more He must know the mind and heart of the mortal who cannot struggle any longer. How He must care for the condition of the anguished child who yearns for peace at last.

I once loved a man with such a troubled heart. I was his

namesake and as a child I used to spend summer days riding on his lap atop a big red tractor on his farm. He would let me pretend to be driving the unruly machine across open fields and down country roads, but in his quiet way he kept his strong hands on the wheel so that I never knew he was guiding me all along. As I grew older, he let me ride in the front of the big farm trucks and told me wonderful stories about happy times and good days ahead. The cab was always dusty, the cushioned seats ragged and torn, the springs poking out, but we laughed and carried on about the beauty of life as though we would never see it any other way.

He was a gentle man and sensitive. Respected by his community, he served on boards of banks and businesses. Invariably he was an advocate of men who could not pay their debts on time, men for whom life was not always filled with happy times and good days.

One Saturday he took me in his old green car into the city to see a movie called,"The Ten Commandments." We wept for joy as the Jews broke their chains of bondage and set out for the land of freedom. The Red Sea parted and they marched across to new life. Charlton Heston's magic was nothing to the miracle my friend explained to me. He helped me to understand the promise that God holds out for all the faithful.

Later I entered the ministry, and he stayed on the farm and witnessed the constant resurrection of life from seedtime to harvest. I studied and came to believe in the God who scattered the stars across the universe and cares for each of us in our darkest night. I came to believe that He will lead us on to morning. My friend never had to study it. For him, it was a way of life.

Last year he slumped into dark depression where no one was able to reach him. He went through the act of living, but he was no longer alive. Though his gentle spirit was never to leave him, his mind shut down and he became imprisoned in indescribable misery. He had no will to be a captive of this world any longer. Like those who had gone before him in the faith, he wanted to break the chains of bondage and set out for the promised land. Just before spring came, he killed himself.

—IN MEMORIAM—
for One Who Took His Life

In his gentle and quiet way, he always understood us. Now, in our turn, we are called to understand him. In the end, that's all that any human being asks of any other: To love, to be loved, and to be respected for living life as he sees fit to live it. Just as he gave so much to so many of us, now each of us can give back to him some measure of care and concern. I pray we will let nothing overshadow the beauty and goodness of all that went before. We must not let the manner of his death deny the dignity of his life, or the faith and humility of his spirit.

When I was very small he taught me the lessons of nature . He was at one with the scheme of the universe, its everlasting births and rebirths. He knew the ebb and flow of things, knew that to find the unfolding perfection of eternal life, we must first cross the river of death. And when we cross that river the Bible says "God will wipe away every tear from our eyes, and death shall be no more, and neither shall there be mourning nor crying nor pain anymore, for the former things have passed away . . ." God has planted eternity in the human heart, and anyone who has worked in the garden and planted in the soil knows that His promise will at last turn into a marvelous and perfect life.

And so it is that some of us look forward to that new life. He was not afraid of it, but rather he embraced it and let go of the cares and values of this world and rushed ahead to meet the new day. Some of us wait our turn. Others hasten to greet the dawn. I believe there was no closer moment of communion between this man and his God than that final, fragile moment when he chose to sever his ties with this life and hold only and forever more to God. What a spiritual moment that must have been between them—what a holy experience with the Divine—that sharp instant which none of the rest of us have ever completely known but which happened to him when he let go and let God have his life.

He did not mean us any harm at the last. He did not want to hurt us. I suspect our grief is the only regret which troubled him. He would not want us to feel guilty or to think to ourselves, "If only I had done this," or "Why didn't I do something more?" When a man has made the ultimate decision about this earthly shell, it is not possible for anyone to change it. There was nothing anyone else could have done. We cannot spend the rest of our lives in remorse or guilt. There is no reason for either. He would not have it so.

None of us here can know of the anguish and pain of the last weeks of his life. It must have been a mental suffering beyond all endurance, something we dare not judge. It only saddens me that we could not give back to him the very thing he gave to us: Encouragement. That was not humanly possible. He was so very much like Barnabas in the Bible. Like St. Paul's companion, this man we mourn never asked for glory but rather he stood humbly on the earth he loved and let others live in the brighter lights. That's why the early disciples named their friend Barnabas, because it means "Child of Encouragement." He encouraged others to go ahead and make their names in history as the famous followers of our Lord, while he stood in the background, content to know that he first planted the seed of faith in so many of their hearts.

He gave his best as a son, husband and father. You were each and all faithful to him and he took strong delight in being faithful to you. I know he would not want his death to scar your lives. Rather he would want the foundation he laid for you to be the beginning of a new life, a strong life of laughter and pride for the whole family. You have a right to be proud of so many things he gave you, and nothing must take that away from you. Most of all—I beg you—claim your right to be proud of him.

I want you who are very young and strangers to death to think about this day in the way God means it to be for us all. Death is not the end of life. It's only the beginning of the completely perfect life which was meant to be from birth, but which can only be realized upon death. Dying is like those nights when you went to sleep in the wrong room, or maybe in the car on your way home, and when you woke up the next morning, you were in your very own room and your very own bed. And then you rubbed your eyes and thought about it. It dawned on you, all of a sudden, that without your ever knowing it, your father came for you in the night and, with strong arms of love, carried you home to the place where you belonged. Death is like that. This death today is like that. In the middle of the darkest night, without his ever knowing it, God came for him with arms of love and carried him home to promised peace.

I think what he would say to us now is this: "Don't weep for me. Weep for yourselves but not for me. I'm okay now. I'm at peace at last. My pain is soothed, That which was broken is bound up, That which hurt is now healed. I'm free. Behold, I am alive forever more. I am a whole new creation. And I will dwell in the house of the Lord forever."

Like so many of you, I owe so much to him. I owe him so much of my faith. I owe him so much of my understanding of the earth and the scheme of the universe. The death of winter, the life of spring. I even owe him my very name.

There's a song he used to whistle which comes home today. His mother taught it to him and, when I was a child, he taught the song to me. I think it says it all.

> Come, ye disconsolate, where'er ye languish
> Come to the mercy seat, fervently kneel
> Here bring your wounded heart
> Here tell your anguish
> Earth has no sorrow that heaven cannot heal.

Amen.

"And now, may the Lord watch between me and thee while we are absent one from another, and may we dwell always in the arms of His love."

CHAPTER 9

When the Triumph Dies . . .

Grief after Violence

LOSING SOMEONE IN A CAR WRECK, fire, flood, plane crash, or similar catastrophe brings with it a particular kind of grief. This is because the death itself is quite unlike that which comes at the end of a long illness or as a result of a breakdown of some vital organ.

Death by violent circumstances is immediate and terrifying. Though a quick death following an accident may have the advantage of precluding prolonged suffering, it brings with it a sharp ugliness which most of us would rather not experience, or have anyone we love experience. No one wants a child or spouse or parents to be savagely beaten to death. We do not want them raped, violated, brutalized, or burned during their last precious minutes on earth. This may have happened at the time of sudden death. For the rest of our lives we imagine what they went through. The scene is sudden and jolting, excruciating and cruel, and we cannot help seeing it again and again. Memory and imagination can torture the griever endlessly.

There is hard anger mixed with it, of course, and it tends to be more bitter than that of people who survive a more "normal" death. For many, there is also the guilt of surviving the wreck or trauma, if they were personally involved, or the guilt that comes from feeling, if they were not, that things might have been different if they had kept the person from being on the scene of the disaster. Such guilt, like the anger, has a sharper edge to it than those stages we have previously rehearsed. So we look anew at the process and power of healing when it must overcome obstacles such as brutality, the memory of horror, the imagination of what the end must have been like for someone we cherished, and the anger, guilt, and depression in the aftermath.

A friend of mine whose small daughter was run over by a car says that she cannot get over the notion that her child was killed like a dog. The death of their daughter is one issue which the parents must survive, and the manner of that death quite another. They will probably never say, when someone asks them about her, that "She died several years ago." Rather, they will always feel the door of death slamming them and they will say bluntly, "She was run over and killed when she was nine years old." And why don't they simply refer to the death the way people commonly relate their grief? Because, in fact, she did not just "die," she was killed. And the impact of their collision with the terror of the universe has left them outraged. Just at the peak of life's good they suddenly feel as if they were gunned down. Or a bulldozer leveled them into the earth.

I found it to be so in my own life. When I was very young a close friend of mine died of a rare disease which took him quickly in the night. I felt that death was wrong and I missed my buddy. But the notion of meanness or some ugly God systematically crushing the human race never entered my mind. So often, since that time, I have thought of Rusty and our tree-climbing together. He never finished growing up in my mind's eye and I still see him today as a twelve-year-old with crew cut and T-shirt. I know his family miss him terribly and, as grateful as they are that he lived, they mourn their loss each day. But we have not felt anything cruel or absolutely catastrophic about the event of his death. He died quickly, quietly, and peacefully.

It was quite different some years later. At the close of high school, on the last day of activities reserved for graduates, another good friend was drowned while shooting the Yellowstone rapids. This time there was more to meet in the confrontation with death than the end of life. He must have suffered horrible panic and wild gasping for air in those last eternal seconds. In my mind there is a definite image of Butch struggling and fighting to live—and all the time he sinks lower and lower into the rushing river. Then his superb body is bashed against the rocks, and he is helplessly tumbled and washed down the roaring rapids like a spent inner tube. I cannot get it out of my mind. My memory of what actually happened, coupled with my imagination of what must have happened, have produced an image which will not leave me. I'm grateful for the rich and meaningful years he had on earth. His happy jumping into every moment of life has remained an inspiration to me. But those last moments of his youth, his life, are fastened to my thanksgiving in a way which seems to keep sucking at the good.

Still later, in the last spring of college, the young woman I had long adored was battered to death in a head-on collision with a truckload of telephone poles. Visiting the scene of the accident clarified what must have happened that rainy afternoon. The incline of the hill was so slight that the state had not painted a yellow line to keep motorists from passing and so Anne pulled into the other lane to move ahead. The hill was, however, just steep enough to keep her from seeing an oncoming vehicle in bad weather. The truck hit her at such a colossal speed and with such an impact that her death was probably instantaneous. Yet every time I recall the life that was hers and our times together I end up thinking of the way it *all* ended. Pictures rack my mind of her trusting innocence and olive beauty being savagely destroyed in the crash. How long she was conscious or how much she saw or what she felt we will never know. I still ask what everyone who grieves a violent death must ask: "What does 'instantaneous' really mean and, in view of the end itself, what difference does it make?" Regardless of what she saw coming or how long she was conscious, it will always be a source of anger within me that such a serene and viable life was thrown so maniacally and brutally back and forth inside that little car; ripped by jagged metal, mutilated and crushed, finally, beneath an overbearing weight. It was six hours before the state police could identify her remains in the wreckage.

We who must incorporate such tragedies into our lives and our faith need, in the process, to find a way to keep going. We give thanks for the goodness and the gift given in the life of the victim because we know that this is an essential hook on which to hang our feelings. Yet we know they did not die as others die, and we cannot make it so. Grateful though we are, we still seethe with anger at the injustice of death for the innocent. They did not die. They were killed.

It is fair to say that these are the times when we resent not only the unaccountable ways of the universe but the lack of understanding of what we are feeling. With all our modern technology and medical advances, people tend to forget that there are uncivilized forces beyond mankind and beyond

control. We have come face to face with more than the
reality of death and we are shocked by what seems mean-
ingless madness. Struggle as we may, how are we to make
room in our world view for what was inconceivable before.
We try to work through our theology until we can at last
come up with a faith which encompasses the insanity of
certain explosions which have neither rhyme nor reason.
It is an intensely personal struggle and it comes just at the
time when the support of friends and relations seems to
come through in inappropriate ways. Fresh flowers and
mass-produced "sweet" cards of sympathy, from the pen of
a stranger who has obviously had nothing worse to deal
with in life than a flat tire at an inconvenient time, leave us
all the more certain that our journey to acceptance must be
walked alone. These efforts of consolation are well intended
and we know that. But they are no less an insult in view of
what has happened. If only someone would come instead to
say "I'm at a total loss for words. I don't know the right
things to say or do because I can't believe it myself. But I
couldn't *not* come. If you feel like talking I'll listen and if
you'd rather change the subject we can talk about it another
time." To say you don't know what to say is more appropriate than to produce stilted phrases which convey no understanding.

Everyone knows, though often we forget, that "It rains on
the just and the unjust." A little rain is tolerable. We can
even take a few bad breaks. But when life begins to bruise
and batter us, when it savagely attacks us without ceasing
and murders love itself, we grow bitter. It's a bitterness
which is hard to overcome. It can only be dismantled in
time, and then only when we sort through our philosophy
and faith, finding there a new perception of our God and
ourselves in the midst of disaster.

Our ancestors were perhaps better at coping with the

ugly side of reality. After all, they were more exposed, more vulnerable, to the harshness and brutality of human life. Nevertheless, at their best and as reflected in their sacred songs and prayers, they met the forces of evil and cruelty with a faith that was shaken at times but not destroyed. The ancient Israelites, our forefathers in the faith, kept seeking—and finding—God in spite of the doubts that assailed them. The enemy within teased the psalmist, "Where now is thy God?" and the early poet sifted through the absurdity that plagued his mind until he found God within and that unfailing Presence became "a song in the night." These early people of God carried that nightsong in the heart through bondage and exile, famine and war. They were not exaggerating when they wrote of their confidence in the Almighty in spite of the fact that at times they could see their whole world crumbling. "God is our refuge and strength, a very present help in trouble. Therefore we will not fear, though the earth be removed, and though the mountains be carried into the midst of the sea. . . . The Lord of hosts is with us; the God of Jacob is our refuge" (Psalm 46: 1–2, 11).

Yet you don't have to look very far to see that these same believers didn't always accept their fate without a fight. They even wanted God to destroy the deceitful, to rid them of the enemy. But when they realized God would not have it so, still they could do no less than register their complaints. They expressed their deepest grief and feelings: "My heart is sore pained within me: and the terrors of death are fallen upon me. Fearfulness and trembling are come upon me, and horror hath overwhelmed me. And I said, Oh that I had wings like a dove! for then would I fly away, and be at rest" (Psalm 55: 4–6). It was a lovely wish, of course, but nothing more. They remained earthbound and learned to live with the justice, as well as the injustice, of life. And this they did, not because they had lost their faith in the midst of life's battles, but because they found it there. They did not write religious pulp out of their experiences but a resounding affirmation of God in the night. Neither did they figure out some divine meaning behind every setback. Unlike their twentieth century descendants, they did not perceive every battle as a test to "build character." Some things they just accepted as the facts of life and were sustained by their inner strength. God did not cause their hearts to be sore pained within them, but they believed that He cared for them in their suffering. This gave them faith enough to keep the faith.

We, too, must find a way to integrate our anger at the scheme of things, the good with the bad, until we are able to do more than just endure life—we participate in it by shedding our tears of grief, sharing our sorrow and anger in the right places and times, and in some divine and mysterious way, holding on to hope.

No matter how hard we try, we shall not make sense of the disaster which has fallen on us. There is simply no sense to be made of it. This is a difficult proposition to accept when we have been raised to believe that all things have a purpose behind them, that they begin and result in reason, and that two and two always total a satisfying four. There are those who need to twist this part or that part of tragedy to make "divine" sense of it all. They want to see God's hand at work so they can articulate its meaning and conclude that everything is just the way it always was: God's in His heaven—all's right with the world. It is easy to understand their need to believe that they have not suffered in vain. And always there are people who feel secretly punished by tragedy. They fear God is getting even with them for something they have done or left undone. It is their just punishment, they think. As foreign as this may sound today, it is yet another attempt to seek divine logic in human disaster.

But it is more realistic to conclude that there is no sense to be found, no meaning to be extracted and totaled up, but only life in its raw, often inexplicable state. Does this reduce all affliction to absurdity? Does this render us existentialists with no sacred connection to the Sustainer of life? Quite the opposite. It raises our pain to the heights once tapped by our ancestors. No trite slogans or pious clichés will comfort us. We shall only be calmed by a faith which not only makes allowances for, but even accepts, the unacceptable. We do not ask for answers. We cannot.

The Jews who were carbonized at Warsaw knew there was no escape from the ghetto or from the minions of Hitler. Yet they kept their faith, not in spite of what they knew was going to happen, but precisely because of it. It is not their mortal victory for which we remember them but for the spirit which refused to be defeated. When all other hope was taken from them, this spirit alone gave them hope. Their only defense was this inner weapon of faith which offered them no easy answers, no "right makes might" and "we shall overcome." They could not use their faith to overcome the enemy or win the battle, but they would at least die full of faithfulness to the Spirit which dwelt within. It was this decision that rendered them heroes in the sight of their brothers and sisters all over the world. In that ghetto they were displaying exactly what Jews everywhere were struggling to feel again: Hope in the midst of hopelessness. Today they are just as dead as the Jews in other places, but they are singled out and praised annually for being symbols of faith and courage and strength. Their community, even in holocaust, lashed out in anger yet kept the great spirit of life.

We can do the same in the face of the dark night which overshadows our being. We can be free enough to explode with rage at what has happened, and, at the same time, keep the faith that the earth rolls on and that we do not stand at the center of the universe a magnet for pity. God holds out a peace for those with courage to go beyond evil. More to the point, we can be consoled by what the New Testament calls *splanchnizomai* ("to feel bowels of pity")—God's caring "at the gut level" for the human condition. The Christian faith centers upon the agonizing death which is the mortal exemplar of this hope in the face of hopelessness, this last question which has no earthly answer, this unseen caring of God in His heart and soul which reaches out to us in all times and places until we can do nothing but commit our spirit into His hands.

The guilt incurred following the destruction of one person or many is largely dependent on the role of the survivor. If you were not in any way involved, your guilt will consist in looking back over life and recalling all those things you have said or done which now seem unforgivable. Try not to chastise yourself for what has gone before and was long ago understood and forgotten.

If you feel yourself directly or indirectly involved, either by having actually been there or by having suggested something which may have led to it, then your sense of guilt will be deeper. This kind of self-negation, in one or many forms, is normal. Chances are, however you think you contributed to the tragedy, your part was only one of many crucial factors that figured in it. You may have enlarged your role beyond all reasonable perspective, taking on more guilt than is rightfully yours. Along with this, and beyond it, try to separate the vital issues until you can see exactly what it is you feel guilty about and how much of that guilt is not due you. You may be holding on to these self-defeating thoughts because you unconsciously relish the awful feeling with which they reward you. It is astonishing how we treasure this comfortable racket of guilt simply because we think we deserve to be punished. In time we not only become accustomed to it, we rather enjoy living with it. It's what we deserve! If no judicial system can rightfully punish us or no other person condemn us, then at least we can have the excruciating pleasure of punishing ourselves. As any amateur psychologist can testify, this hurtful game is played by millions of otherwise perfectly sensible people. Something there is inside us that seeks incrimination against ourselves for so many wrongs we have committed. Or think we have. In light of the disaster which has suddenly surrounded our thinking, what better way to punish ourselves than by using minor mistakes to build a full case against us? If and when we should decide to live free of this age-old racket, we have only to think through the incident and analyze our role until we understand the dynamics that led to the various decisions and actions. We must do this as often as is necessary until we genuinely accept our humanity and our completely forgivable capacity for error. Gradually the rattling will become a murmur which we can rise above to a life of grace.

Perhaps you have what is known as "survivor's guilt," that awful feeling that you, too, should have perished. The fact that you're alive leaves you with haunting questions why and how and for what purpose, and the gnawing suspicion that you have no right to exist. If others were killed, why weren't you?

This kind of guilt was brought home last year when a

nightclub in Kentucky exploded, burning to death members and guests. Those who escaped have since confessed a terrible shame that they got out alive. Should they have fled and left the others? Did they block someone's exit? Should they have stayed longer to help? What stroke of fate drew the invisible line that made all the difference in the world? While it is normal to ask such questions, we must remind ourselves that there are no answers. In every tragedy involving more than one person there is only a breath's difference, an invisible line, between those who live and those who die. One second you were exchanging casual pleasantries with another mortal being of flesh and blood like you, and in the next your vis-a-vis vanished into nothingness. Disappeared off the face of the earth! You caught a glimpse of the precarious glass wire that separates the living from the dead, the present from the absent, and it snapped. Intellectually, it is possible to accept the fact that life exists and death must happen, but it is rare for them virtually to coexist and then separate so vividly that nothing again can ever seem the same. The moment is too abruptly real to be true. But it was, and is, the truth. While some might take spiritual comfort in concluding that there must have been some heavenly intent inside the fragile, brittle difference, others more realistically accept it as the plain—and horrible—fact of the moment.

I often marvel at the narrow escapes we have routinely without realizing it. An actual accident raises an acute awareness of our rescue from death, but how many accidents are avoided simply because we took a different highway or left home a bit earlier? This sort of escape is no less a rescue. But because it is usually unapparent we do not suffer from survivor's guilt or spend our nights agonizing about the meaning of our existence. Neither do we flog ourselves for just being alive. So, while it's right to claim that all of us should sense the wonder and gift of our lives, that we should celebrate every breath we draw and every step we take, it's untrue that we were spared when somebody else was not. This is too great a burden for anyone to assume.

When this kind of survivor's guilt overtakes you, remember that you are no better or any more important to the heart of God than any other single human being. The Almighty has not played favorites; neither has He organized a cruel holocaust as a means of picking and choosing, giving and taking. This is plainly not the work of the God of love. You and I have not been singled out and selected to live as a part of some divine scheme, any more than others have been "culled out" and killed to satisfy divine justice. I do not find any basis in our faith for deciding that we have been saved because there is some special job which only *we* can do. If we truly believed that, we would nearly go insane trying to find that job and trying to appease God. Nothing would satisfy our magnificent obsession. We would, in fact, lose our sense of purpose along the way.

It is natural that survivor's guilt should produce a desire to do something important with your life. Rather than chase after some mysterious justification for your right to be, try being thankful that you lived through the tragedy and that you once again have a place in the universe. You don't have to earn it and neither do you have to prove anything. Yet you are rightly concerned with having your life count. To paraphrase the Hebrew poet, you've had reason to consider the number of your days and thus you've applied your heart unto wisdom. You might begin by helping all of us to be keenly and constantly aware of the fragile nature of our heartbeat and so to perceive existence as a condition of being which gives us a chance to contribute. While the fact that we must die (and that you know more acutely than most) cannot be our *only* motivation, it can surely remind you that you are better for finding the value in a day than for wasting it.

Severe depression is another long lasting and normal reaction following a major trauma. Most of us have been taught that if we look for the good in life, we will find it. We've been conditioned happily to believe that if we spend ourselves in doing good, good will return to us. Yet now, without deviating from that principle, you've been struck down and bashed against the rocks. The very meaning of life seems confused and perverted. So you stare silently for hours on end, or lapse into memory failures in the middle of conversation. Your span of concentration will not allow you to read or focus your mind for any long span of time. You keep wandering away from the present because you've had a terrible revelation and you don't know how to express it or cope with it.

Try not to give in to it. After a few minutes "off duty" from the present, return and take your part in it. This rotation on and off will keep you in touch with the continuity of life. Depression of vast magnitude can throw you into despondency and even bed for the rest of your life. In many direct and indirect ways, it may render you helpless and pitiful. Some minor physical ailment can be psychologically enlarged until it actually cripples you. I've seen it happen often and almost always from a desire to give up the fight. You've got to function again, to get one foot in front of the other and begin to find your way back into the flow of the river. You can't avoid the river. You're better off trying to move into it, wading carefully to evade the shock, and then learning to flow with it again. Holding back will do no one any good. It will only deepen your depression because you are no longer moving with the rest of creation.

When we spot a child on the playground who is hurt and

whimpering, all alone and far away from the laughter of the group, we know the only solution to his pain is to fold him gently into the activities again. Soon he will be a full participant in the community. Laughter will bubble up from his soul—as a response to his new-found happy feelings—just as it does from his playmates. But the longer he refuses to join in, the more certain it is that his friends will stop calling for him, and he will never take the initiative of rekindling the spark of happiness. Perhaps your despair leaves you on the sidelines, alone and out of touch. If you make the effort your companions will reach out and include you in the circle again. If not, you can expect the circle to drift farther and farther away.

Redirect your hurt to give you a hope you never knew before. A friend of mine had a way of expressing it after he emerged from the valley of the shadow of death, the tragedy that left him mentally and physically devastated. He said, "I've died once. Nothing on this earth can frighten me again. Nothing can surprise or overpower me again. Nothing can keep me from fighting for what I believe to be important. Now I'm convinced that I can survive anything, by God's grace—even mortal death." This can be your creed, too. In spite of all that has gone before, you have a leverage for living which few people possess. But you must seize it. Even if you cannot explain it, the secret knowing in your heart can give your whole life the quality of the eternal Spirit.

Is all this to say that we are to try to forget the horror we have seen, to live as though it never happened? On the contrary, we take up life again because we have seen the very worst of it; we have felt the glass wire snap and we have survived. Scarred and ripped and broken-hearted, we have nonetheless endured.

Some particulars, however, must be mentally blocked if we are to keep on surviving. It is too much now, to remember everything. With a rhythm all its own it will come to you and each time you can deal with some portion and then put it away and think of other things. I know one woman who realized, months after her tragedy, that she was trying to remember too much and all at once. Her psychiatrists advised her to try blocking out most of the memories. This may sound like strange advice from physicians trained to help us deal with the past openly. But it's a sound approach for surmounting disaster. What you can never forget, you must integrate into the total recovery and healing process. Some aspects need to be pushed back until their time, and then put away forever. Block what you must, integrate what you can. Then blend together the bad with the good until you arrive at a peace which is uniquely your own and which few outsiders can understand.

It has been said that real Tragedy with a capital "T" is that experience over which there is no triumph in this life. I believe it. All grief brings with it at least some of that kind of Tragedy, especially the grief which follows a massive disaster. So many things can never again be the same and nothing on earth can change that. The wound will never completely heal. We have no choice, if we are to survive with sanity, but simply to find a way to live with it. And that's not simple. They say that time heals all wounds. They're wrong.

Yet there is triumph to be found if you who have eyes to see. There is sheer endurance, for example, in the full face of adversity. That in itself is a triumph of the human spirit. Then there is the victory of love, unseen and intangible, which friends bring to you as a silent offering and presence. If you can accept it and fold it into your grief, you will have achieved another triumph. The gradual healing of the tormented mind and weeping soul, the new-found capacity to accept the disasters of life as an eternal reality, the gift of seeing the sunrise again and feeling its sign of victory—all these are indicators of mortal triumph in the midst of defeat. You cannot hope for a complete victory, a total triumph over all that has happened. You cannot regain the split second before the delicate glass wire snapped, or the way you perceived life until then. But you can at least piece together enough of the good within and around you to become whole.

Once put together again, you will gain that marvelous knowing that this new kingdom is forever.

CHAPTER 10

The Trumpets Sound

My sword I give to him that shall succeed me in my pilgrimage, and my courage and skill to him that can get it. My marks and scars I carry with me, to be a witness for me, that I have fought His battle who now will be my rewarder.

So he passed over, and all the trumpets sounded for him on the other side.

John Bunyan
Pilgrim's Progress

I HAVE HAD MY EXPERIENCE with a virtual holocaust, one of those Tragedies over which there is no complete mortal triumph. Yet in our own way and in the light of what might have been, we are salvaging what triumph we can, and each day that we take it up again we are finding ways to call that triumph good—an inner victory worth every inch of the struggle.

The airlines called one Sunday afternoon to notify me that my aunt and uncle were on board one of the ill-fated Jumbo Jets that crashed head on just hours before on the tiny airport at Tenerife in the Canary Islands. It was not known if there were any survivors. For hours the catastrophe remained an impossibility in my mind. Throughout the rest of the evening I watched the news and received more phone calls from the airlines. Something told me that my indestructible Aunt Beth would somehow survive. "She's my born survivor," I told myself, "too full of stout resolve and determination, raw guts and will power to succumb." Something else made me suspect that my gentle, sensitive uncle would not make it. True, he had been strong and resourceful enough to command his way through many situations. A vice admiral in the United States Navy, he was so in touch with the universe that he could find his way home across the dark ocean by following the stars, and this he had done time and again as commander of fleets in the South Pacific. But he was also an officer who had sailed in full acceptance of his promise to sacrifice for others and go down with the ship.

The Department of State called the next morning to confirm that Vice Admiral Walter E. Moore had perished in the crash. My indestructible Beth, in critical condition, had somehow survived.

Because of a bomb scare on Los Palmas, their destination, several 747s had been rerouted to the unequipped airport. Once on the ground, confusing messages were issued from the control tower to the cockpits, and from one airliner to the next, until no one was quite certain what anyone else was attempting. All we know at this point is that one Jumbo Jet took off from the end of the runway and, just as it gained maximum momentum, blasted broadside into another 747 as it, too, headed for takeoff. In a timeless second which no one remembers, both aircraft were smashed against the ground and began exploding, engine after engine. Six hundred people were killed, some instantly and some slowly, and more were burned beyond hope, mutilated and maimed for life.

We now know that my aunt and uncle began making their way towards the one small opening in the burning craft. It was ringed with jagged metal knives and the wounded passengers who had an ounce of life left in them had to hurdle high-back seats, one after the other, fighting the hurricane of debris, pushing and shoving through lifeless bodies and hurling metal, praying with every last breath to make it to the splintered hole. Feeling his hand slip from hers, my aunt turned to see her husband's head hemorrhaging from the blow of a hot metal knife. He was still alive but it was clear that he could not continue. Uttering his last command, he pushed her out the opening and turned to help people behind him.

Some of the survivors reported being saved by my uncle. We do not know how much longer he lived with the mortal wound, but we know he died doing what he had to do. The great Admiral Nimitz once praised him as "the toughest, meanest, most unbending officer in the United States Navy." But those whom he saved were later to describe him in gentler terms. He had no choice, by his code, but to do what he did—to save his beloved and then to save the lives of total strangers. It was more than just the duty of my admirable admiral; it was his nature. And that same nature, I'm persuaded, has found its way home by the stars. His voyage has been blessed by God and our noble sailor is home from the sea.

My aunt found herself standing on the upper slant of the wing tip and peering down some forty feet to the ground. That's roughly the equivalent of looking down from the rooftop of a three-story house. Then, from a standing position, she took the first step towards the only option left. She jumped. Doctors were later to label the injuries sustained in that landing as both internal and external. Her bones and joints were described as "broken, fractured, disintegrated, pulverized, and powdered." Then more passengers began jumping on top of her and the jet engines on her side of the craft started to explode. The landing gear gave way and the jumbo inferno collapsed around the screaming survivors. Those who could fled for their lives, leaving the helpless victims behind, while others began lifting and pulling the wounded from beneath the wreckage. It was a microcosm of life. The elements of selfishness and sacrifice which are dormant in us all came to the surface in those minutes and were to become etched in the memories of those who lived.

One of my aunt's many recurring nightmares is of lying on the ground and watching the passengers fall from the wing on top of her. Then they ran away. Still she could see the opening which held the only hope for her husband. If he did not emerge from the plane, she preferred to be with him. In spite of her instincts, she was at that time and for a long time afterwards, sorry she had survived. In the same dream she visualizes a man wearing a dark green sweater standing on the wing above her. He looks down at the flaming rubbish on the ground and is afraid to jump. Those who have made it shout "Come on, jump! You can do it! Jump!" As much as he wants to plunge to the ground, he is paralyzed with fear. What has happened inside that man just at that moment?

Two island teenagers, perhaps thirteen years old, climbed through the debris and began dragging her away from the constantly exploding furnace. We never learned their names but they were indeed two young Davids who took on a flaming Goliath at the risk of their own lives. Then an old man carried on where they left off, hauling her as far as he could. His clothes were in flames. The purser of the crew, Dorothy Kelly (who was later to receive two medals for heroism) found the two of them inching through the smoke and began to help. It was at this precise instant that a passenger snapped a photograph which was published around the world on the front page of newspapers and the full color double spread of magazines. In the foreground of the picture is the knotted threesome agonizingly supporting one another, and around them are other survivors fighting to save themselves and those nearest them. Some are wandering mindlessly across the field, stunned. In the background is the sunken Jet which has smoldered into a rotting shell. Faintly visible in the photograph is the man in the green sweater, still standing on the wing and afraid to jump. Some five to seven seconds afterwards, the final explosion ripped apart the fuselage and the last of the Jumbo Jet blew off the face of the earth. The pleasant holiday and the lives of six hundred human beings were all over.

Bleeding and holding themselves together, survivors ran or crawled from the fire. My indestructible Beth—always a woman of grand presence and dignity—was immobilized on her back. Using the palms of her hands for leverage, she forced her body up the stubbled field and away from the fiery furnace. My hunch was right when the airlines first called. She's my born survivor.

Public disaster is invariably accompanied by curious onlookers, bureaucracy, thieves on the lookout for loot, and a maze of excuses why the obvious cannot be done. When so many people become involved and so many officials take charge of evacuation, while investigators and the financially involved start descending on the scene, the survivors become almost incidental to various objectives. Families of the victims could not land on the island as long as wreckage was left strewn across the runway. Investigators for an assortment of private interests needed to examine carefully what was left of the Jets so as to be prepared for law suits. This is predictable, whether the tragedy be a car wreck or a plane crash. There were forms to be completed, fortunes of international corporations to be protected and, eventually, victims needing to be flown home to American hospitals.

The physicians and nurses in the small island hospital did a fine, though primitive, job of preparing the patients for the long trip home two days later. Like so many others trying to make contact, I tried every imaginable channel to get through a message to the hospital. My friends in the church used endless connections to break through the maze; they turned up eager comrades at the Pentagon, the State Department, the telephone company, and the airlines. When you multiply such efforts by the number of friends and relatives trying to gain information on particular patients, you see the impossible magnitude of the job. American linguists were unable to understand the unusual dialect of the island people. So it was that more language experts were added to the relay system through Madrid. Burgeoning chaos was exacerbated by the extreme variations in time zones between California, where the flight originated, and Tenerife—where it ended. Whether it's a minor accident down the street or the worst disaster in airline history across the world, a single human being is nearly overwhelmed by unexpected obstacles.

It's good sense to let your friends help you through this aspect of the ordeal. They want to do something constructive and it's likely that after hours fighting the meshes of entanglement, you will be less rational than they. Never will I forget one beloved friend who quietly arrived late the first night and, without asking permission or giving advice, simply brought his toothbrush and camped out by the phone. He was there when I woke in the morning.

Only two words were relayed across the ocean regarding Beth's condition: "Very bad." The authorities in this country assured us that no message could be gotten through for some time. Later I was to find out that one doctor in the small island clinic was rushing past the emergency switchboard when he heard a familiar case report being radioed back to the United States. Realizing he had just left that patient in deep shock and critical condition, he went back into her room and attempted to pronounce my name. Then he added "'Merica.'" She understood.

If there was hope of breaking through red tape for the welfare of a desperately ill woman, there were other mountains to be overcome. It could not be decided which agency should be responsible for the return of the survivors: the American government, the Spanish government, or the airline. Further word came to a few of us that our next of kin were quite possibly not able to endure the trip on the ferry ambulance which would take them to another island airport so they could be flown home. What were we to do in such an event? "Stand by." We stood by all that day and night. The following afternoon we were advised that the U.S. Air Force was transporting the victims home in a special Jet rigged with stretchers stacked five high. Would my aunt be on that flight? "Stand by."

A kind gentleman in the State Department made radio contact with the ambulance Jet as it was departing the island. He telephoned immediately. My precious cargo was secured on the last deck of stretchers, in the tail of the plane, on the top tier. Minutes later an embarrassed official from the San Francisco office traced me down to say that he had temporarily lost information on the victims. Did I have any idea where they were and when they were due to land in the States? He needed to pass along word to the next of kin on the West coast. "Tell them they're now in the air," I said, "they're due to land on the East coast at 1:00 in the morning." When I asked why he should be calling me about the whereabouts of the survivors, he confided: "Reverend, we figured out twenty-four hours ago that you were getting more advance information through your church than we were getting through Washington."

Bob James, whose son we had recently buried, took charge of the journey to the military base. We sat looking out the back windows of the car and said nothing. Suddenly I was paralyzed with fear and I did not know how to tell him. I was deeply afraid to see my aunt again. I had nothing to give to her who had lost everything, nothing to say to her who had spent three days in the flames of hell. Finally I told Bob that I understood the real reason for his tears when his son was almost dead. He had nothing to give to him, as his father, nothing to say, nothing to offer, no way to heal the very son he loved. He was such a powerful man in the ranks of this world, yet he was reduced to tears in the face of what mattered most. It is frightening to discover that we're only human, I told him, and to be so helpless when we're needed most. Then I reminded him of the exact night when we were riding down that same turnpike shortly before his son died, and he was talking about the same thing. Only I didn't completely understand then. "Well," I finished, "now I'm a crybaby too."

Someone met us at the gate and ushered us to a special glassed-in waiting room on the runway. The relatives of the people disembarking on the East coast were gathered and waiting. It seemed odd that none of us talked to each other.

My only guess is that we really did not want to know whether this stranger or that had lost a parent or child or lover. We just sat in silence and watched the black sky. An officer called us to the desk. He told me our destination was San Francisco and the best hospital the military had to offer for casualties of war. I was to board as soon as the plane landed for refueling.

An hour later the man called us back to the desk. Her condition had worsened in flight and she could not continue the journey. She was to be taken off when the Jet put down. "The doctor on board doesn't think she can hold out much longer."

"Listen, can you do something fast? Can you radio the pilot to get word back to her that I'm here, waiting for her? Just tell her to hang on a little while longer and we'll make it. This sounds irrational but she can make it if she knows I'm here. We always slay our dragons together."

He radioed the pilot. A nurse was sent back to climb the ladder to the top tier and deliver the message.

It was 3:00 in the morning when life lost the shadow of the crucifixion and took on the light of the resurrection. This time there was no stopping it. The grey and white Jet with the red cross on the tail touched ground with brilliant lights flashing in all directions. They were home! In the darkest night came the sign of hope: that in spite of human error and overwhelming holocaust, in spite of all the barricades and obstacles, the stone was being rolled away. With light beaming down the runway and engines roaring that wondrous sound, the stone was being rolled away.

Ambulances were wheeling up to all sides of the monster as it taxied to a full stop in front of us. Beth was taken to a nearby small hospital and we were driven to another waiting room. This time there were fewer families and I wondered what happened to the rest of them. Among all those anguished cries coming from the emergency room, I recognized hers. I slammed my fist against the wall and Bob grabbed my arm. "Just be glad she can still scream."

When I came to her side I knew instinctively that it didn't matter what I said, just so long as she understood we were together. Nailed and suspended in all manner of machinery, dried blood caked on her head, the terror in her eyes told me she was very near insanity.

"Listen, you turkey, settle down. We've got a hell of a dragon in front of us and I'm not going after him alone. Whether you know it or not we're in the pits of New Jersey and this is no place for a lady to be seen. They're waiting for us in San Francisco and we've got to get there. I'm telling you we'll make it but you've got to hang on and help me." They started rolling her away. "So get your vital signs in order because we're going on to the promised land—in spite of those silly pajamas they put on you. You've got the rest of your life to tell me what hurts but tonight you've got to help me with the damned dragon."

Three days later we landed in San Francisco and were taken to the hospital. The chief surgeon informed us that it would be days before they could attempt surgery, and the operations would be strung out over a period of years. She was not then strong enough to go under the anesthetic.

We talked quietly through those next days. She taught me that it's never too late to tear down an old faith and reconstruct a new one which is fit to do battle with the evil of life, to endure it, and to survive with nothing but God's nightsong in the heart. Hers was to become a faith which those who have never hung on the cross beside Christ, unjustly persecuted for no good earthly reason, can fully understand.

The psychiatrists and chaplains came and went in utter disbelief at the sight of her and at the sound of her remarks. When it was better to keep silence, she did so. One chaplain gently took her hand and assured her, "The Lord never gives us more than we can carry. You just remember that." When he left the room, my spirited patient turned to me and whispered through the oxygen mask, "If he knows so damned much about it, why doesn't *he* carry it?"

One of the unspoken problems of those who survive a collision with the ugliness of reality is there seems no place to register our complaint. The empty universe does not answer back and we have no one with whom to negotiate a better deal. We're infested with horrible feelings but we have no place to bring them. How can we lash out at someone who made a human error? The people at the controls never meant so much damage and death to so many. The driver of the other car was drunk, perhaps, and your child paid the fatal price. The drunkenness doesn't excuse anything, but how on earth can we vent anger against someone who wasn't even sane at the time? Life dishes out life with no respect to persons. For believers, our only consolation is that God Himself took on the absurdity of it all, innocently, and had the spikes of life's thorns and nails driven through him. He hung there first so that we do not have to hang there alone.

The victims of pain and cruelty understand. Beth began to strengthen me with her raw faith, just as she was strengthening others who came to help. Early on the morning of surgery a young and nervous orderly came in to introduce himself and to tell her that he was taking her down eight floors to the operating room.

"Take me away," she said to the orderly, "and you do the driving of this contraption. If you want to take the elevator

I'll go with you. And if you want to take the stairs that's perfectly all right with me. We can survive anything."

Hours later I was on the midnight flight bound for New York, it was Easter morning. Flying East I realized that I had been a witness to the story of Easter. Jesus said: "Greater love has no one than this, that a man lay down his life for his friends." We had commemorated the last act of my uncle who had done exactly that. He had saved others, too, but himself he could not, would not, save. The military world will remember him for being a strong commander of men. But I shall remember him for saving the life of the woman he loved. In so doing he gave her a new birth of faith and hope and love.

It was a Tragedy over which there is no triumph on this earth. But still we take heart in the quiet triumph within: the triumph of divine love and humanity, a triumph of compassion and care, of people sacrificing their lives for one another, helping one another. Out of the ashes of the holocaust has risen a phoenix of treasures, stories of undying love, courage and compassion, devotion to one another. After that terrible crucifixion, those mortal survivors symbolized the very story of Easter.

Someone, that divine Someone whom no one has seen, threw us all out of the burning plane and gave us life. Broken and wounded though we are, all of us, we cannot let our hearts be hardened to the miracles around us. We've got to work to save each other, helping one another, risking our own security for the good of the unknown neighbor who is trapped and in trouble. Immobilized and hurting, pulverized and powdered, we've got to use what little leverage we have and pull ourselves, push ourselves, along the pilgrimage.

We will cry when we must, laugh when we can, but we must never give up on each other or on ourselves. It takes the mortal lesson of the crucifixion and the resurrection to bring it home to the heart. Material possessions, in the end, are worth nothing. We need only each other and our God. Together we shall slay the dragons that would keep us from the promised land.

Leaning back and listening to the whine of the engines, I ached for sleep. A gentle peace from somewhere settled over my mind and I let go of the holocaust and faded into thanksgiving with the Easter dawn. "The Lord is risen. He is risen indeed."

Hallelujah. Amen.

Fronie and Clancy

IT IS OUR NATURE not to want to live so long or die so alone that there is no one left to care. We deserve someone to grieve our demise—at *least* one. If it is true that when a clot of earth is removed from the main the whole of the continent is the lesser for it, then how much more our human absence should be marked. It seems somehow right.

I have presided at services which were grandiose in final fanfare—trumpets and orchestra, bagpipes and organ, candlelight and roses. I have seen the sanctuary of our church filled and overflowing with honest friendship and the spirit of deep love. We have marked well the completed lives of our comrades. At the end of each journey, we have joined together again and again to sing praises of thanksgiving.

But for Fronie Simpson, it was all quite different. I first met Fronie several years ago when I went to call on her companion, Ruth. The electrical power had gone out that night and Ruth led me into the living room by lantern. Over in the corner, a candle glowing across her distorted face, was Fronie. Severely retarded since birth and never educated or trained even up to her own capacities, she had been given to Ruth like a wild animal more than twenty years before.

Ruth taught her to do so many miraculous things, considering that she could not understand the meaning of words or even the intent of the most basic instruction. They went over every movement time and again until Fronie arrived at her own way to repeat it. Ruth taught her to sit up at the table without having to be strapped in a chair and, later on, to eat with the proper utensils. Though she never learned to bathe herself or put on her own clothes, she did discover the delightful sensation of a hot shower and the bouquet of fine perfume. These she motioned for every morning and every morning Ruth would perform the ritual of getting her friend ready for another day.

The night I was introduced to Miss Simpson she was doing what she always did: rocking wildly in her chair, laughing uncontrollably, pulling at her grey hair and petting her cat, Clancy. I tried making polite conversation with Fronie but Ruth assured me she had never uttered a word in her fifty five years and "It's not likely she'll start tonight." It crossed my mind briefly that Teacher had performed marvels with Helen Keller, so why wasn't it possible for Fronie? Then the key difference struck me: Helen Keller had a mind, and a keen one at that. Fronie had almost none.

Ruth and I visited the hours away and Fronie never stopped rocking and laughing or pulling and petting. The power never came on again either. To say the old house had character is a euphemism. To say it was falling into shambles is the truth. That night it seemed haunted with spirits and I confess that Fronie didn't help much.

Clancy climbed down every so often and walked around the room. Then she jumped back in her friend's lap and purred away while Fronie resumed her heavy stroking. Ruth told me that Fronie and Clancy had been rocking in that same chair for fourteen years. Before that, Fronie

rocked alone. Her raving and carrying on seemed like familiar comfort to the old cat. In their own ways, they were
equally at odds with the human world, but Clancy had the
distinct advantage. She could clean herself and forage for
food and she was seldom confused or frightened. Fronie, on
the other hand, was totally dependent and she was never
quite sure if the movement around her betokened friend or
foe. She had not the instincts for survival nor the sensitivity
to people that Clancy had. It was the cat, Ruth said, who
gave Fronie "feline feelings" as to the danger or safety. If
Clancy signaled that all was not friendly, Fronie would
follow the cat out of the room. But if Clancy liked the guest,
the two of them would continue laughing and purring in the
rocking chair.

That meant Clancy liked me. Her instincts must have
told her our paths would cross in the years ahead so we
might as well become friends. The cat was smarter than I,
for it never occurred to me that we were only beginning a
story which would take us beyond the grave.

The three of them lived without words in that old house.
In many ways they lived in escrow because the house had
been left in a peculiar trust and was to be inherited by
whichever woman outlived the other. Even Clancy was
named in the will. If the house should be sold during the
lifetime of the cat, the purchaser had to agree to keep the
animal or provide a new home which would be agreeable to
the executor of the estate.

Every day except Sunday Ruth went to work as a wait-
ress to earn enough money to feed and clothe Fronie and to
take care of Clancy. She needed money to fix the roof and
replace the gutters, too. Over the years I watched her pour
all her savings into the dilapidated house, never complain-
ing but always thankful that the three of them had a shelter.

When the furnace gave out, she worked extra hours to buy a new one. When the stove broke down, she came up with the cash to replace it.

Fronie had no concept of time. At 8:00 o'clock each morning she was positioned at the window and stayed all day watching for Ruth to come home from work. In her nervousness she constantly rubbed the wooden window frame until she finally wore down the grain and left ridges and valleys which led to secret places only Fronie could feel.

Ruth devised an ingenius scheme to rest Fronie's legs while she waited through the long hours of the day. She hung a cuckoo clock next to that window. When the bird came out of its house to sing, Fronie learned to sit down with Clancy and rest for fifteen minutes. Then, surprised by the bird again, she stood up and watched for her companion. And so it went, all day long. The cuckoo sang and Fronie sat down. The cuckoo sang and Fronie stood up.

People in the church chipped in to help with labor and expenses to keep the house going. Ruth was a proud woman and we took care not to undermine her dignity. But some people suggested that Fronie would be better off in a mental hospital with full-time company, a peer group of her own. Ruth would not hear of it. She knew the laughing soul could never adjust to another environment, that she would die without her companion and her cat.

Two years ago Ruth was in a car wreck returning home from work. It left her incapacitated and unable to care for her friends or for herself. We made arrangements to have her flown West to an institution near her family. The attorney for the estate informed me that because of the strange trust there were no available funds to provide for Fronie and Clancy. The house and property would first have to be sold.

In the meantime, I kept asking, what were we to do with

them? The law seemed to have no room for such a question. I called several good mental hospitals and they suggested we make an appointment to bring Fronie in to be interviewed. Budging her out of that house would be impossible. Holding her down in the chair for an "interview" would be a catastrophe. It became increasingly clear that Fronie could not pass anyone's admissions test. When I mentioned the delayed financial proposition they immediately referred me to the county home. That dismal prospect became our only hope.

I wanted to explain to Fronie that it would only be temporary. Just until we could sell the house and afford something cleaner and better. She never understood. The station wagon from the county hospital pulled in the drive and the attendants wrapped Fronie in restraints and dragged her out of the house. Her laughter turned to tears and hysteria. They locked her in a ward with a hundred other women in a pavilion which is off limits to the public. It's reserved for the constant hollering and hell of madness. I was allowed to stand outside the gate and look into the vast gymnasium which had nothing but metal beds at one end and bars on the high windows. Some of the women even hung onto the top of the gate with fierce strength, dropping like crazed insects when the attendant rapped on the bars with a stick. He tried to explain to me why it was not possible to go inside and talk to Fronie.

While people from the church immediately started cleaning up the house and getting it ready to sell, realtors began rummaging through the old place to estimate its worth. In all the fury it took me a week to recall that the cat was to be sold with the house—and suddenly Clancy was nowhere to be found. We learned that someone had locked her in the basement for safekeeping, and that was the last we knew of her. We never knew how long she had been down there or how she got out, but some time during the week Clancy broke free. My only hope was that, like Fronie, the cat knew secret ridges and tunnels in the walls of the house.

Late one afternoon a call came from the county hospital. Ruth had been right: without her companion and her cat, Fronie died.

The woman from the hospital informed me that many of their patients were entitled to a county burial. It was the *least* they were entitled to, I thought, and it was obvious that she would be carted off to some potter's field and dropped like an unwanted and unclaimed burden. I told her to stand by for further instructions.

There was never any question but that church members would pick up the expenses of a decent burial and a granite monument. Yet we needed something a bit more special for Fronie. Neither a county burial nor one bought by strangers seemed appropriate. I began calling the sensitive funeral directors I knew who might take an interest in our plight. One of them phoned back to offer his services, and that of others, free of charge. He said the only problem remaining was a burial plot. Fronie didn't have one and the cost to buy into the new cemetery would be exorbitant.

I quickly assured him that he needn't worry about the cost of that property because Fronie wasn't going near it. A few miles from her old homestead, surrounded by an iron fence and carefully maintained by gardeners, was the Père-Lachaise of local cemeteries. The names on the tombstones read like a social register of the dead. There were stones that dated back to the Revolutionary War. It seemed somehow just that Fronie be buried in the best of company. She had fought her own battles and paid her dues in this life. She should be surrounded by the spirits of those who also understood the struggle for freedom.

"But that's just not possible," my friend at the funeral

home said. "It's almost closed territory. Nobody qualifies for that one any more." We both chuckled at the absurdity of it.

Chuckling on, I said, "When it comes to being dead, Fronie qualifies." We argued lightly until he began to understand what an important creature this was in the kingdom. He had never realized that her ancestors were so prominent. "In fact," I concluded, "you can trace her heritage all the way back to God. Surely *that* should count for something."

It counted. He made a few more phone calls and then confirmed the exact hour when no one would be on the property. I knew he had quietly asked his associates and the respective unions and legal authorities involved with the cemetery to turn the other way, just as I was asking him to do. It was better not to press the bureaucratic jungle he had cajoled and untangled. In the meantime I drove to a garden nursery and found the owner more than happy to contribute a bunch of the ground cover called periwinkle. It is deep green and fast growing and puts out blue blossoms in the spring.

We met the next morning and walked the cemetery to search for the right setting. Overlooking a soccer field where laughter could be heard echoing up the hill, and near the corner of the graveyard where a little white cottage stood guard, we found it. Between two tombstones we started digging. One marker bore the name of an old and respected family, and the other was finely landscaped and beautifully cared for. I was sure the gardener wouldn't mind trimming the periwinkle when it invaded the wrong plot. He was equally sure to be delightfully amazed at such a burst of evergreen. And his very calling meant that he would never step on the small flowers or crush the leaves.

We finished digging the small grave and knelt to place the urn of ashes in the ground. I paused in silent thanksgiving for the care she received in this world and for the grand attention she was bound to get in the next one. For Fronie's sake, I hoped, heaven would begin each day with a hot shower and fine perfume. It was the style to which she was accustomed and if anyone deserved to spend eternity in style, it was Fronie.

Filling in the grave I was overcome by a sense of irony. At the end of her life there was no one left to grieve and no one to attend to the last affairs save for two near strangers. How like the last hour of the Nazarene. The faithful disciples had gone their way and it was two near strangers who claimed the body and buried Jesus in a garden tomb. It never fully came home to me until that moment how God had completely encompassed humanity in the crucifixion, how He had identified totally with loneliness and death. Not only had He taken on the final experience and defeated the last enemy for all of us, He had at the same time included even "the least of these" in His miracle. They were always His favorites. To the outcast and the lame, the blind and the suffering He ministered first. And last. Even in the last affairs of Christ, God was speaking a final Word of understanding and eternal love over the lives of the least of these.

The periwinkle served as the only marker. Planted in the fresh earth and watered with spring rain, we left it to take on festive life again every year. My friend and I agreed that no else need know what gave birth to the blossoms. It would be a secret that would leave the gardener dumbstruck and the heavens rocking with gladness. But we were not the only ones who knew.

Two years later at a friend's dinner party, I was listening

to a bright young couple regale the guests with stories of having fixed up their old house. It was on the edge of a cemetery. As they continued their saga of remodeling and moving into the house beside the tombstones, it became apparent just which cottage they inhabited. Shortly after they moved in, they said, they adopted the first cat that cried at their door. There were to be other animals after that one but none so old and sick as Clancy.

"Clancy?" I asked. "How did you decide on a name like Clancy?"

"We didn't," said the wife. "We took the poor thing to the local veterinarian because she was so emaciated and he recognized her immediately. He said her name was Clancy and she belonged to a retarded woman outside the village. He checked into it and found out the lady had died so we took the cat home with us and expected her to do the same. We fed her milk through an eye dropper and somehow she began to revive. The vet said she had to be at least seventeen years old then and she's still going strong today!"

Everyone at the table expressed amazement at the age of the cat and someone suggested it was proof that these animals indeed have nine lives. The conversation turned to pets and their antics, their instincts and strange habits. I waited for the evening to be over.

Early the next morning I dropped by the cottage and put my hands on the unbelievable. There was no doubt of it. Clancy had found her way to the cemetery and taken up residence next to Fronie. I told the story to the young people and none of us could fathom its implications. We had heard of such things but nothing like it had ever touched our mortal worlds. I walked with them through the graveyard and showed them the evergreen.

As I recounted more of the past, they told me more of the

present. Clancy still had her comforts. Practically every night she cried until one of them rocked her, petting her into that familiar purr. During the day she played in the cemetery.

I saw the couple again a few weeks ago and they told me of their plans. "Even a cat can't live forever," the husband reasoned. "So we've decided there's only one place to bury her when she dies."

Until then, Clancy will spend her nights being rocked and lulled to sleep. And she will spend her days playing between the tombstones and rolling in the periwinkle.

The place, of course, will be our secret.